PRESIDENTIAL CAMPAIGN QUALITY

REAL POLITICS IN AMERICA

Series Editor: Paul S. Herrnson, *University of Maryland*

The books in this series bridge the gap between academic scholarship and the popular demand for knowledge about politics. They illustrate empirically supported generalizations from original research and the academic literature using examples taken from the legislative process, executive branch decision making, court rulings, lobbying efforts, election campaigns, political movements, and other areas of American politics. The goal of the series is to convey the best contemporary political science research has to offer in ways that will engage individuals who want to know about real politics in America.

PRESIDENTIAL CAMPAIGN QUALITY
INCENTIVES AND REFORM

Bruce Buchanan
University of Texas at Austin

UPPER SADDLE RIVER, NEW JERSEY 07458

Library of Congress Cataloging-in-Publication Data

Buchanan, Bruce.
  Presidential campaign quality: incentives and reform/Bruce Buchanan.
    p. cm.—(Real politics in America)
Includes bibliographical references and index.
  ISBN 0-13-184140-8
  1. Presidents—United States—Election. 2. Political campaigns—United States.
I. Title. II. Series.
  JK528 .B83 2004
  324.7'0973—dc22

2003017718

Editorial Director: Charlyce Jones Owen
Acquisitions Editor: Glenn Johnston
Assistant Editor: John Ragozzine
Editorial Assistant: Suzanne Remore
Director of Marketing: Beth Mejia
Marketing Assistant: Jennifer Bryant
Prepress and Manufacturing Buyer: Sherry Lewis
Interior Design: John P. Mazzola
Cover Design: Kiwi Design
Cover Photo: Jeff Mitchell/Corbis
Composition/Full-Service Project Management: Kari Callaghan Mazzola and John P. Mazzola
Printer/Binder: Courier Companies, Inc.
Cover Printer: Phoenix Color Corp.

This book was set in 10/12 Palatino.

Real Politics in America
Series Editor: Paul S. Herrnson

Pearson Education LTD.
Pearson Education Singapore, Pte. Ltd
Pearson Education, Canada, Ltd
Pearson Education–Japan
Pearson Education Australia PTY, Limited

Pearson Education North Asia Ltd
Pearson Educación de Mexico, S.A. de C.V.
Pearson Education Malaysia, Pte. Ltd
Pearson Education, Upper Saddle River, NJ

10 9 8 7 6 5 4 3 2 1
ISBN 0-13-184140-8

*For Stephanie, Doug, Katie, Jackie, Moe, Heidi,
and the rest of the Buchanan clan*

Contents

PREFACE

Americans hate politics, and a hardy band of good government advocates would like to do something about it. Admittedly, this is not fresh news. Indeed, it may no longer even be a particularly welcome subject for discussion. The 2002 campaign finance reform legislation, for example, the latest achievement of a longstanding reform tradition, played to a largely indifferent national audience. For many, the ills of politics and how to fix them have been rehashed too often to be interesting. Others, noting that political reforms rarely actually fix anything, have simply abandoned hope. To them, unsatisfying politics, like air pollution, is something we just have live with. Taken all together, so many have become convinced that they have heard it all before that it is getting hard to write on this topic without sounding hackneyed.

So why am I adding another book to the stack?

Because the very durability of this much-worked issue shows that something is stuck. Important business remains unfinished. A stubborn, hard-to-resolve contradiction vexes our politics. This, and not some naive idealism, is what keeps the issue alive. It won't be laid to rest until we figure out why the kind of electoral politics that most Americans want—principled policy debates that clarify what is truly at stake in every national election, followed by high rates of voter participation—seems perpetually beyond their reach. The sources of our frustration can be elaborated as follows.

THE PROBLEM

What generations of experts, critics, and ordinary people have wanted is elections structured to give voters clear choices among policies as well as candidates, so that they can better understand and protect their interests, as representative democracy intends. This requires that candidates stick to the important issues facing the nation, avoiding both diversionary topics and off-putting campaign styles. It requires the print and broadcast journalists who cover and report the election to pressure the candidates in interviews and press conferences to stay focused on what really matters, and then to write and talk more about their qualifications and issue positions than about their campaign strategies. And it presumes that there are attentive citizens who, while preparing themselves to vote "smart," are also willing to punish departures from the public interest script at the polls, seeing to it that a political process that is supposed to protect their interests actually does so.

What we usually get instead, of course, is vastly different from any of this. Candidates do what it takes to win, which often means avoiding or distorting controversial high-priority issues, inflaming and exploiting divisive "hot button" issues, pandering to target voters, and digging up or manufacturing dirt on opponents for use in attack ads. Network television news executives, driven by sagging ratings, offer less and less campaign coverage during prime time and fill that reduced airtime with overhyped accounts of the campaign wars that mention issues only when they are being used as weapons in the fight for power. Journalist David Broder, a longstanding critic of *status quo* politics, adds to this picture by slamming "politicians who buy popularity with tax cuts and special-interest subsidies, while postponing action on important public needs," and journalists "who put profits and ratings above their obligation to provide substantive information and analysis of public issues."* Meanwhile, those eligible to vote, who increasingly find this spectacle irrelevant to anything they care about, are moving past anger to indifference, as more and more of them simply tune the whole thing out.

THE PARADOX

Clearly, the reality is very different from the wish. It is so different, in fact, that we should wonder why aspirations so out of touch with reality retain any power over the popular imagination at all. Why do so many critics cling to so apparently unrealistic a vision of the desirable? Why don't they articulate achievable goals instead, goals that might put the redemption of politics more easily within reach? My answer, detailed in the first chapter, involves the righteous anger felt by critics like David Broder when politicians show contempt for bedrock democratic values. But whatever the reason, this idealistic vision has proven to be just as durable, if not quite as pervasive, as the political reality it wants to change.

---

*David Broder, "One Man's Reminder That Gift of Freedom Comes at a Price," *Austin American-Statesman*, 6 July 2002, p. A-15.

The Plan of the Book

This is the paradox that I use this book to examine. The point of the exercise is to see if it might finally be resolved, one way or another. To move past our frustration with election politics, we must either find a way to adjust our aspirations downward, thereby eliminating our chronic and not entirely healthy discontent with the political *status quo*, or figure out ways to establish the kind of political practice we want, something we have so far, despite repeated efforts, been unable to do. What follows is my effort to identify a course of action that makes sense, and to suggest how to make it happen.

I start with my core hypothesis: The paradox springs from a fundamental design flaw. In order to function as intended, any representative democracy needs an *incentive system* that will elicit the necessary behavior from candidates, the media, and voters. The reason we get a political reality so different from what we want, as I argue in Chapter 1, is that the incentive system that we have simply does not support what we want. Instead of evoking a policy debate, it sparks an unprincipled fight for power. Instead of attracting, informing, and inspiring voters, it drives them away.

This is a self-defeating state of affairs. It has fueled both chronic political discontent and nearly two centuries of efforts to reform the electoral process. But because we have overlooked the importance of incentives, we have usually misdiagnosed the problem, and the reforms we have put in place have not worked. One reason for our misdiagnoses is that the occasional campaign does manage to beat the odds and meet our expectations. In Chapter 2, I analyze two such campaigns: the 1960 Kennedy-Nixon contest and the 1992 Clinton-Bush-Perot confrontation. Both featured substantive policy debates followed by increases in voter turnout. Why? Because special circumstances like the threat of war faced in 1960, the economic anxiety that formed the 1992 campaign, or the passionate, policy-driven political conflicts that stamped historic elections like 1800, 1824, 1864, or 1936 can sometimes *alter the mix of incentives* in ways that fire authentic debates that fully engage an electorate made attentive by problems and crises.

But when crises do not arise, the result is usually self-serving candidate exchanges that clarify no national priorities or choices and spark little voter interest. Only rarely does a candidate believe it is in his interest to "go substantive" despite a lack of voter demand, as George W. Bush chose to do in 2000. More typical is "going negative," as in the mean-spirited campaign of 1988, or avoiding controversial but high-priority problems by "offering voters candy," as in the evasive campaign of 1996. Both are described at length in Chapter 3.

Does all this mean that only crisis can improve the quality of presidential campaigns, and then only temporarily? The fact that two centuries of reform have failed to generate any sustainable increases in voter turnout or policy emphasis implies that the answer is yes. But there is another possibility worth considering. It is that past reformers have misconceived the nature of the problem. Unless we are willing to accept the political *status quo*, on the grounds that crisis improves the quality of campaigns when it really matters and that quality can otherwise safely be ignored, we need another approach to reform. That is the path I recommend here.

I develop a new approach to reform in the last four chapters. The rationale for doing so is in Chapter 4. There I review evidence that shows how voter participation and campaign policy focus *contribute to the success of the government*, and why, therefore, the longstanding efforts to increase both cannot be dismissed as merely a "good government" impulse that is without pragmatic grounding. The fact that consistently better campaigns would be *useful* to the polity in various ways is why we should not be content to rely solely on crises, but should instead seek to institutionalize improvements through more effective modes of reform.

The first step toward improvement is suggested in Chapter 5. Having established that the point of substantive campaigns followed by high voter turnout is to *increase the chance for an impact on policy*, the next task is to show how it can work. The vehicle need not always be a presidential policy mandate, as is often argued. It can instead result from what I call a *policy signal*, a broader mobilization of political will that depends less on who wins the election than on the degree of consensus generated among voters, media, and candidates about what the main national problems are and what might be done about them.

What forced policy signals in the cases I review was not candidate initiative, nor media crusading, but *voter demand*. When crises spark good campaigns, it is because voters insist, and because under certain circumstances their wishes cannot safely be ignored. The purpose of Chapter 6 is to spell out those circumstances. Not every expression of the public will commands the respect of candidates or reporters. As I show with examples, only citizen demands that constitute *credible threats* to their political and economic success are likely to get their attention. To achieve that, the demands have to be clear, stable, and backed by the threat of punishment.

A worthy if ambitious aim for campaign reform would be to equip voters to use credible threats to evoke both real public policy debates *and* civil campaign practices from candidates in noncrisis circumstances. An electorate motivated to do *that* would be anchoring an incentive system that supported the democratic ideal. The problem, of course, is how to give people not moved by fear a reason to move without it. That is why I return in the last chapter (Chapter 7) to the problem of motivation. It is inattention to motivation that has bedeviled most past electoral reform efforts aimed at citizens. For example, there have been many expansions of the right to vote, but turnout has never increased as much as expected. The reason is that it is one thing to expand the franchise, and quite another to get people to show up at the polls.

I deal first with the easy part, namely, describing a plan for readying citizens to assume expanded responsibility. The task is straightforward. First, continue to remove the barriers to engagement and voting, as many reforms have already done. Second, make a more comprehensive use of a wider range of both existing and yet-to-be-tried campaign-season opportunities to inspire interest and action. And third, add to the citizen portfolio the skills and techniques needed to make routine, coordinated demands on candidates. All well and good, we might agree. This is the sort of thing that is found in many idealistic reform proposals that don't work. The hard part is to give the American people, who now suffer from an incentive deficit that leaves half of them unwilling even to show up at the polls, a compelling reason to do even more.

The only conceivable way for *that* to happen is to revive a practice that has all but died out: instilling in each new generation of Americans an old-fashioned attitude—*civic duty*. This is no longer a priority in America. That is why the attitude is likely to be little more than an abstraction to many readers of this book—especially younger readers. But civic duty is a sentiment that can be taught, and that, if well taught, can function just like an incentive—in the same way, for example, that getting elected or making money are incentives. We see civic duty at work today when millions of older voters trudge to the polls despite the fact that there seems to be nothing really in it for them. But there *is* something in it for them: the satisfaction of doing something they are convinced they *should* do. A strong sense of personal obligation to the political process, and a willingness to act on it, are the drivers that, once in place, can impel voters equipped with the right skills and techniques to compete with candidates in the setting of campaign agendas.

Finally, the structure of this book reflects a simple theory of what I call "campaign quality." The theory emerged from a decade of research and analysis of presidential election campaigns that I and others undertook on behalf of the John and Mary R. Markle Foundation. Most of the evidence cited in chapters to follow is drawn from the 1988, 1992, and 1996 Markle presidential election studies. The surveys were conducted for the Markle project by Louis Harris and Associates in 1988 and by Princeton Survey Research Associates in 1992 and 1996. The 1988 media content analysis was by Luce Press Clipping Service; 1992 and 1996 media and candidate content analysis was by the Center for Media and Public Affairs.

ACKNOWLEDGMENTS

The impetus for this book was Lloyd N. Morrisett's 1988 invitation to direct what became a series of Markle Foundation presidential election studies. My thanks to Lloyd for his continuing friendship and support.

I also thank my audience of graduate and undergraduate students whose reactions have helped shape the campaign quality argument. Seminar and classroom presentations eventually became conference papers, edited book chapters, journal articles, earlier volumes, and now this book. I have benefited greatly from the comments of the many panelists, colleagues, anonymous reviewers, and editors who critiqued one or more of these writings along the way.

Finally, I appreciate the professional advice and encouragement offered by Niels Aaboe. And I am grateful for the confidence shown by Prentice Hall Editorial Director Charlyce Jones Owen and *Real Politics in America* Series Editor Paul S. Herrnson and his Series Editorial Board. Needless to say, any remaining errors are mine.

Bruce Buchanan

PRESIDENTIAL CAMPAIGN QUALITY

THE PROBLEM

DEMOCRACY'S INCENTIVE SYSTEM

Presidential election campaigns are the centerpiece events of American democracy. That means the quadrennial exchanges between candidates, media, and voters open the best available window on the state of electoral politics. With clocklike regularity, they show how well the American political experiment is working each time around. Regrettably, the process now inspires more critics than defenders, and the critics are not impressed. The reason, as I suggested in the Preface, is that the kind of voter-friendly, policy-rich campaigns the critics want are—perversely—just the kind they are least likely to get. Tenacious expectations for *good* campaigns are matched, and usually trumped, by equally stubborn incentives that yield *bad* campaigns instead.

This conundrum springs from a design flaw—namely the failure to engineer a system of incentives that can reliably deliver in practice what representative democratic election systems imply, indeed promise, in theory. Not that the subversive candidate, media, and voter incentives now in place were deliberately conceived and consciously installed; the fact is that they merely evolved. But wherever they came from, the incentives operating now simply do not support the kind of campaign practice that Americans want. I will make this case by comparing what the critics regularly demand of each of the actors in the electoral triangle (see Figure 1.1 on page 2) with an assessment of the incentives that usually push and/or pull those actors in decidedly contrary directions.

CAMPAIGN DYNAMICS

Consider the dynamics of the typical campaign. Candidates move first, testing themes and messages for their attractiveness to voters and media. They try to create "news" (e.g., a succession of fresh scenes, audiences, events, high-profile support announcements, and policy speeches) through a ritual of traveling and speaking. They supplement their road shows with "paid

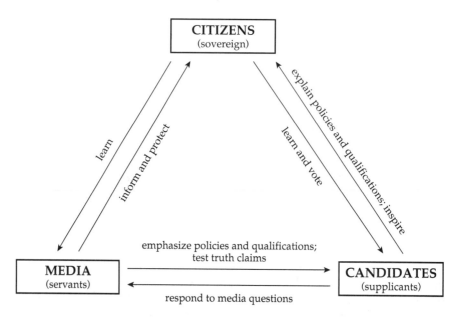

FIGURE 1.1 THE ELECTORAL TRIANGLE

media" (i.e., television advertising) both to protect against free media distortions and to reach larger audiences that don't watch the news.

For their part, media editors and reporters sensitive to markets and competition edit candidate shows in ways designed to get attention. Audience responses to both campaign and coverage are extensively monitored through polls, focus groups, and other devices, often leading to message and coverage adjustments. Candidates and media also monitor and react to each other.

It is this seeking and adjusting to feedback, especially target-audience feedback, that makes campaigns interactive, as depicted in Figure 1.1. It is also what gives voters the power to shape campaigns by their reactions. What comes of this dynamic depends on how the circumstances of a particular campaign affect the behavior of the actors. Except in crises that galvanize voters to make demands, those circumstances usually find candidates and media struggling just to craft messages and styles that are emotionally compelling enough to move what will usually be a sluggish and indifferent audience.

WHAT CRITICS WANT

Critics want substantive discussions of important national problems and their possible solutions, and they want a strong majority of eligible voters to show up at the polls for every election. It is easy to identify the actor behaviors that can raise the policy stakes and increase voter turnout. Candidates need only propose and explain solutions to important national problems to elevate those problems in the public mind, like 2000 Democratic-nomination candidate Bill Bradley tried to do with health care, and like Republican nominee George W. Bush did with his Social Security privatization plan and his proposal to use existing "faith-based" private organizations to help government provide services to the poor. It is equally easy to identify things that spur turnout. Campaigns that make direct contact through telephone and door-to-door canvassing and direct mail always get more voters to the polls.[1] Unusually interesting candidates—Ross Perot, Colin Powell, Jesse Ventura, and John McCain are recent examples—can also attract enough attention to increase engagement and turnout, while less exciting personalities, like 2000 Republican-nomination candidate Steve Forbes, cannot.[2]

News media can build attention to any campaign, and also stimulate voter turnout, simply by covering it extensively. In 1988, when only 28 percent of available post–Labor Day television airtime was devoted to campaign coverage, turnout barely reached 50 percent. In 1992, available airtime devoted to the campaign neared 40 percent, and turnout jumped to 55 percent. In 1996 coverage dropped back to 20 percent of available time, and turnout fell to 49 percent. There were factors at work other than TV coverage, such as economic anxiety and the novel campaign of Ross Perot, to help boost the 1992 vote.

But it is also true that the networks made self-conscious efforts to enhance their coverage that year:

> ABC ran 21 lengthy "American Agenda" features on where the candidate stood on major issues; CBS ran "Eye on the Campaign" interviews with major campaign players; and NBC's "America Close-Up" offered the sort of contextual and thematic coverage often missing from daily campaign trail coverage.[3]

Media can also help voters protect their interests. By drawing attention to the policy commitments of candidates and repeating key information, news organizations increase the likelihood that the audience will truly understand its choices. Media also discourage candidate manipulation by exposing it. And they can stop fueling public distaste for politics by not overcovering the things that aggravate it, like candidate attacks.

What, finally, is to make candidates and media behave like this? Vigilant citizens, who reward good behavior with votes and market share. When voter-consumers make their wishes clear in sufficient numbers, candidates and journalists have little choice but to respond.

LINK TO CRITICISM

We know that this is what critics want because its absence is what they complain about. It is, in other words, the lack of such good campaign behavior that sparks the most familiar complaints about electoral politics. And it is important to notice that the criticism often has a righteous, indignant edge to it. This is because it is inspired by an implicit *normative* vision of how things *should* be; a vision that is rooted in democratic theory. For example, many critics, especially voters, have long been unhappy with the candidates' tendency to duck tough issues and to attack opponents. The implicit message is that candidates *should*, on moral grounds, address real issues in civil tones.

Others, especially media researchers, complain about overcoverage of the daily campaign horse race and candidate conflict at the expense of issues[4] and the growing tendency to substitute the faces and voices of journalists for those of candidates in campaign coverage.[5] Implied here is that media *should*, again on moral grounds, let candidates speak for themselves, offering coverage that more closely mirrors reality, except when stressing things that help voters, like repeating useful information. The idea seems to be that the audience is *entitled* to accurate information in a form it can use.

Still others worry most about a detached and politically ignorant citizenry[6] that hates politics but sees fixing it as somebody else's problem.[7] While some political scientists argue that mass political ignorance is both rational and cost-free, many critics cling to the belief that the ignorant risk sabotaging their own interests.

The critics voice a remarkably durable vision of how campaigns ought to work. But as any casual observer knows, the actors rarely live up to the vision. As I suggested earlier, that makes the resilience of the vision surprising. Why do such seemingly unrealistic expectations endure despite their negligible impact on the real world? *Because they are rooted in strongly felt values.* The expectations seem to spring from *conviction*; from what is for many an impassioned belief that representative democracy should be about protecting the interests of citizens first, and those of power-seekers and media conglomerates second. To many critics, this has clear implications for the kind of political practice that is necessary and right in an authentic democracy. As journalist David Broder shows by his choice of words, unhappiness with politics as usual can be strongly felt indeed:

> No one can go to Eastern Europe in this season of its liberation, as I have just done, and come home uninspired by the power of democracy as a universal ideal. It would be grotesque, at such a moment, to watch without protest the strangulation or distortion of democracy in the United States—which symbolizes successful and sustained self-government to so much of the world.[8]

Still, the special power of democratic ideals is not always appreciated, and sometimes the idealistic are scorned for their naivete:

> So here comes another crowd (the Project on Campaign Conduct, sponsored by the Institute for Global Ethics) lecturing everyone to play politics by the Marquis of Queensbury Rules. . . . They want every candidate to sign a Code

of Election Ethics. Their model (includes such) promises as: "I will avoid demeaning references to my opponent and demeaning visual images of my opponent." And "I shall not use or agree to let third parties use subtle deceptions, half-truths, falsifications. . . ." Not to be flip, but what planet have they been living on?[9]

But even cynics can occasionally be moved to lament the absence of political standards. The next excerpt, like the first taken from a *Wall Street Journal* editorial, shows this, and concludes that agreed-upon codes of political conduct are, in the end, essential:

> Despite Mr. Dooley's adage that politics ain't beanbag, there have to be conventions and limits somewhere.[10]

If standards are so important, why aren't they more consistently enforced? Because those with the enforcement power—voters—care so much less than those who resist: candidates.

ACTOR INCENTIVES

Voters hang back because half or more don't feel they have enough at stake to take the trouble to get involved. Those who do turn out are often ill-informed about what is truly at stake in any particular election. That makes it easier for candidates, who are willing to do whatever it takes to win, to get away with murder.

DEREGULATED CANDIDATES

Candidates are forced to deal with reality. The most enduring candidate reality other than tough competition is the lack of regulation. The United States has the least regulated political environment among the advanced industrial democracies. The First Amendment prohibits any significant restraint on what candidates may say or do, as of what news media must cover. This rules out decisive measures used elsewhere, such as England, to discipline candidates by banning political advertising, or significantly controlling its contents, or requiring participation in debates or discussion of issues as the price of access to the airwaves.

Candidates enter this deregulated world with everything to lose and much more at stake than either journalists or voters. That more than anything else is what gives American politics its hard edge. Candidates are free to worry mainly about coming in first, and able to go to great lengths to make it happen.

To deploy a viable campaign involves a daunting collection of tasks. First come financing and staffing. The 2000 winner, George W. Bush, raised more money than any previous presidential candidate in history, and assembled what was regarded as the strongest team of campaign and policy advisors in the race. Next is a strategy and a message to fit the political situation. The 2000 Bush message, "Compassionate Conservatism," was designed to soften the mean-spirited, pro-business Republican Party image. The idea was to offer centrist voters a safe alternative to Clinton's vice president, Al Gore. Then the plan must be road-tested and adjusted to events "on the fly." That is exactly what the 2000 Gore campaign had to do in response to challenger Bill Bradley's unexpected early success at portraying himself as presidential, and Gore as without vision. That is also what Bush and company believed they had to do, by veering to the right and attacking opponent John McCain in South Carolina, after he scored a one-sided triumph in the New Hampshire Primary. In short, the brain trust must continually try to outmaneuver an equally determined opposition in a protracted struggle.

They also must contend with a zealous pack of journalists who, intentionally or not, can produce stories that hurt the campaign. That was why the 2000 Bush group complained about the media's obvious infatuation with Arizona Senator John McCain[11] and encouraged stories about McCain's hot temper. Finally, candidates have to extract a sufficient number of votes from primary and national electorates that are exceptionally diverse, very expensive to reach, and hard to move. The low turnout figures in virtually every recent election bear this out.

These hard realities breed combative outlooks. Opponents, media, and voters are all fair game; different kinds of targets in an all-out war. High-stakes competition promotes both novelty and hardball. Modern lore and tradition—shaped by the most aggressive winning efforts—the Kennedy campaign of 1960, the Nixon campaign of 1968, the Bush campaign of 1988, and the Clinton campaign of 1996—celebrates innovation, guile, and audacity, constrained only by usually very tolerant voters. At their first post-election encounter, 1996 loser Bob Dole complained bitterly to winner Clinton about the latter's "dishonest TV ads that suggested that the Kansan wanted to gut Medicare. [Clinton] smiled, and replied, 'You gotta do what you gotta do.'"[12]

Certain media and voter habits increase the likelihood of candidate strategies that lower campaign quality. The relevant media habit is to overemphasize the contest. The focus on the horse race magnifies the benefits of being ahead and the costs of being behind. This, in turn, increases the desperation of trailing candidates, making them more likely to attack opponents (e.g., Gore and Bush in 2000; Forbes in 1996), to demagogue inflammatory issues (Bush II in 2000; Bush I in 1988) to fuzz the truth (Clinton in 1992), or to promise the undeliverable (Dole in 1996), all out of desperation.[13]

The voter characteristics that encourage sulphurous campaigns include tolerance, ignorance, and indifference. Tolerance signals a green light to ignore limits and restraint. Ignorance encourages lying. And indifference encourages the use of emotional wedge issues and of repetitive advertising to move poll numbers. The cost of advertising increases the penetration and influence of big-money interests.

Voter ignorance and media aggressiveness together invite and justify candidate deception and spin control. For example, voter ignorance made it possible for candidate John Kennedy to "invent" a missile gap with the Soviet Union, which Kennedy used in 1960 to attack Nixon for softness and lack of preparedness.[14] Woodward-and-Bernstein-style investigative journalism pushed self-defensive spin control to new levels of artfulness in the Reagan, Bush, and Clinton campaigns and administrations.

Issue Evasion and Confusion Campaign deception takes many forms, but most relevant here is the evasion or confusion of issues that campaigns might otherwise help the voters to understand and the political system to address. Studies show what political professionals have always known: that candidates can control what voters do and don't know. In one study, incumbent Senate candidates who made their positions on a small number of issues clear increased the accuracy of voter perceptions of those positions. But as incumbents added more issues, voter awareness declined. Attacks also reduced voter awareness of the issue stances of those attacked.[15]

Under what conditions do presidential candidates choose clarity or evasion? Clarity is the choice when the stance is expected to help (e.g., Bob Dole's 15 percent across-the-board tax cut proposal in 1996) or when failure to be specific will hurt (e.g., 1992's candidates knew they had to spell out their economic policy proposals or else). Clarity can also be the strategy of choice in an uphill race that the brain trust believes cannot be won without bold policy moves. That, said Bush strategist Karl Rove at a 2000 election debriefing held at the University of Pennsylvania early in 2001, was why Bush put very specific and highly controversial proposals on Social Security, tax cuts, missile defense, and federal financing of private religious charities on the table. The Bush high command thought that Gore would win unless Bush could change the dynamic by impressing the voters with his policy vision and political courage.

Avoidance or ambiguity is a feature of every presidential campaign. Even when candidates advance bold proposals, they rarely disclose potentially embarrassing details like accurate costs, or implications for other priorities. In 1992, for example, both Bush and Clinton advanced bold proposals that omitted many such details, a fact pointed out in a highly critical front page *Wall Street Journal* story.[16] Evasion is likeliest when the issue is controversial, but not yet of wide public concern (e.g., how to finance the inevitable Social Security or Medicare fix).

Ducking issues the next president will probably have to address amounts to deception by omission, something candidates do regularly.[17] Candidates feel they have ample justification to avoid proposing unpopular measures like tax increases or spending cuts even when they make good policy sense. They point to examples like Walter Mondale in 1984 and Bruce Babbitt in 1988, both believed to have incurred the wrath of voters as presidential candidates by daring to propose tax increases, even though increases were later judged necessary and enacted. Most candidates now believe they must avoid too-specific discussion of just the sort of difficult, "no win" issues that campaigns could theoretically help to resolve. Laying out a realistic blueprint for addressing tough problems is thought to be political suicide for a candidate with a real chance to win. Thus, the 1988 party nominees avoided serious discussion of either the federal budget deficit or the looming need for a bailout of the savings and loan industry. The 1996 candidates did the same with Social Security reform. Though journalists typically point out such evasions during campaigns, only rarely are voters moved to put pressure on the candidates to respond. Particularly when the candidates collude, there is often no political price to be paid for evading "no-win" policy controversies.

The most effective recent use of an evasion strategy was to divert public attention from a focus on big national problems by introducing a steady stream of relatively small-bore, low-cost, and noncontroversial symbolic issues identified by focus groups as favorable to the candidate's electoral prospects. That was the approach taken by President Clinton in 1996, when his reelection campaign platform avoided issues like Social Security and Medicare reform, instead emphasizing "bite-sized" proposals such as school uniforms and V-chip technology.[18]

The difficulty of motivating a detached public inevitably invites candidate appeals to the self-interest of particular groups and to emotions like greed, fear, prejudice, and anger. Targeted policy appeals, such as support for obsolete weapons systems important to regional economies (e.g., obsolete jet fighters made in Fort Worth, Texas), or tax cut proposals made when the economic policy justification is suspect to nonpartisan opinion, rarely address the most pressing national needs. That wastes the campaign's potential contribution to getting real problems on the radar screen. Emotional appeals, such as television advertising that covertly triggers racial resentment (e.g., the use of black rapist Willie Horton in Republican ads in 1988), attacks against the demerits of opponents (e.g., Steve Forbes assailing George W. Bush in the 2000 primary campaign for raising taxes in Texas, or George W. Bush implying in New York Primary ads in 2000 that John McCain opposed research on breast cancer) or efforts to exploit fear of loss of valued government programs among target voter groups (e.g., the Clinton "Mediscare" ads of 1995 and 1996) are standard candidate practice because of their value in the fight for votes. They may work. But many voters dislike them, and some tune out because of them.

Candidates sometimes deliberately seek to alienate specific groups of voters. Political consultant Ralph Reed, formerly of the Christian Coalition, made this point in a recent National Public Radio interview. Modern politics, he said, is increasingly a function of "niche marketing." Tactics that drive voters away can be just as valuable as those that attract them, because to reduce voter turnout in select groups is to reduce the proportion of votes needed for preferred candidates to win.

Some argue that attack ads do not necessarily hurt voters, that ads can be contentious, argumentative, and confrontational—i.e., can display characteristics that many would call "negative"—while still being accurate and informative. In this view, only distortions, exaggerations and outright lies are never legitimate.[19] The 1996 Clinton campaign advertising strategy may be a case in point. But as the conflicting testimony that follows suggests, it can be hard to get agreement on the fairness or legitimacy of any particular attack ad strategy.

The Clinton Ad Campaign   According to Clinton strategist Dick Morris, ". . . the key to Clinton's [1996] victory was his early television advertising."[20] The ploy was to fly "under the radar" of the national media by starting very early (July 1995) and by advertising only in key states outside the major media markets. This enabled the Clinton ads to avoid media notice while driving home the differences between the president and the Republicans on issues known to favor the president, like the ban on assault rifles, and Clinton's opposition to proposed Republican budget cuts in Medicare, Medicaid, education, and the environment.

These ads mixed comparative and attack features that were informative, stressing the actual policy differences between Clinton and Dole as well as attacking Dole positions known to be unpopular. Were they legitimate? According to the *Wall Street Journal*, they contained:

> just enough distortion to be credibly damaging. In grainy black and white, the Clinton spots showed a nefarious-looking Bob Dole next to a glowering Newt Gingrich who were supposedly "slashing" Medicare—though in truth only about as much as the bill Mr. Clinton signed into law a year later. The ads violated every promise [campaign reformers] want candidates to make.[21]

But according to Dick Morris, the ads were "factual, emotional and highly effective. . . . [Morris admitted that] [a]ny thirty-second ad on the budget is an oversimplification of complex questions. But we were quite meticulous in our choice of words."[22]

This disagreement shows that it is hard to define or apply a fairness test that all would accept. The ads did contain information potentially useful to voters. But the Clinton campaign managed to evade media scrutiny that might also have been useful. There was, in addition, an element of Clinton hypocrisy in later approving Medicare cuts like those attacked in the ads. The important question here is not whether particular uses of such tactics can pass some abstract test devised by experts. It is whether the tactics confused people about what was at stake in policy terms, and discouraged them from voting.

The research evidence on the impacts of "negative" political advertising on candidate vote share[23] or on voter turnout is inconclusive. Attacks seem to mobilize partisans, but in some studies tend to depress voter turnout among Independents, who now comprise more than one-third of the electorate.[24] Another study turned up no systematic relationship between advertising tone and turnout over a series of presidential elections.[25] Still, voters regularly tell pollsters that they dislike attack politics and some claim that it discourages them from voting.[26] At a minimum, it reinforces the well-documented public distaste for candidates, politics, parties, and government.

MEDIA INCENTIVES

The major television networks and the major national and regional newspapers that devote significant resources to election coverage are the main sources of widely available information about national problems and candidate plans for addressing them. Their nonpartisan status positions them to offer unbiased information in the midst of highly partisan candidate debates. They also enjoy unmatched access to mass public attention. Near-monopoly control of the airwaves and print space means that news organizations have more opportunity even than the major candidates—who must fight for "free" media attention and buy advertising from the same organizations—to influence voters' grasp of the national agenda and the shaping of their own policy priorities.

But like candidate incentives, media incentives, particularly the profit motive of the executives who control the networks and the career drives of on-camera reporters to express their professional values and to scoop the competition, also work against high quality campaigns. Specifically, these incentives discourage both turnout and policy focus in four ways: (1) by reducing the total amount of television coverage devoted to presidential campaigns; (2) by devoting more airtime to reporters than to candidates; (3) by using reporter airtime to disproportionately cover and criticize the horse race and candidate conflicts, especially attacks, relative to policy; and (4) by trivializing the treatment of policy in the limited coverage time allocated to it.

Limited Campaign Coverage   Largely for economic reasons, the networks have sharply curtailed all categories of presidential campaign coverage. In 1992, the nightly average airtime for campaign coverage was 24.6 minutes. In 1996 and 2000, it was down to 12.3 and 12.6 minutes, respectively; about four minutes apiece per night.[27] This wouldn't matter if the network audience turned to other sources of campaign information, and there are other sources. It is often noted, for example, that the supply of thorough and substantive media coverage is more abundant now than ever before, with the proliferation of 24-hour cable news outlets like CNN, Fox, CNBC, and MSNBC. Are cable outlets building audiences as network coverage declines? Until the 2000 election, when for the first time polls showed a big increase in the number of people saying they watched cable television for election news, the answer was no. The average voter still relied mainly on network coverage. The cable campaign news audience may finally be growing. But 25 percent of the American public is still not on cable. And many who are use it primarily for entertainment viewing rather than for political news. Most important is the fact that the ratio of average nightly network news audience to cable news audience is still about 20 million to two million, or ten to one.[28] Therefore, declining network campaign coverage means less exposure and less opportunity for the far-larger network audience to develop enough interest in the campaign either to absorb information about the policy stakes or to encourage voting.

Reporters over Candidates   Increasingly, it is the faces and voices of journalists rather than presidential candidates that bring the campaign to the mass television audience.[29] "If you actually add up the [campaign 2000 network coverage] airtime, journalists talking about the campaign accounted for 74 percent. . . . Candidates actually shown speaking accounted for 11 percent of the airtime. . . . The time that presidential candidates get to address the American people is measured now in eight-second bursts. . . . When [Republican presidential candidate George W.] Bush went on Letterman, he got more airtime in a single block than he got the entire month of October on all three network newscasts combined. . . ."[30] Why does this matter? Because it allows reporters to dominate the most authoritative source of nonpartisan information about the candidates and their qualifications, driving candidates to inherently less credible soft-format talk shows and highly partisan paid advertising. That would not be so bad if journalists used the time to explain and compare candidate proposals. But as we see next, they do not.

Horse Race and Conflict   They use their time instead to dwell on the ups and downs of the daily campaign. Table 1.1 (on page 12) shows the distribution of network television campaign coverage during the fall presidential campaigns of 1988, 1992, and 1996. (Data for 2000 are not as complete, so I report what is available in the text that follows rather than in the table.)

The six coded categories in Table 1.1 were imposed on a priori grounds in order to capture both the most typical emphases (e.g., horse race, candidate conflicts) and those that are most facilitative of policy signals (e.g., issues). By "most facilitative," I mean information available on the most

TABLE 1.1   MEDIA COVERAGE CATEGORIES: 1988, 1992, AND 1996

COVERAGE CATEGORIES	1988[1]	1992[2]	1996[3]
Campaign horse race	36%	30%	48%
Candidate conflicts	21	17	35
Candidate qualifications	19	7	1
Policy issues	10	31	37
The electorate	10	7	12
The media	4	7	4

[1]Conducted for the Markle Project by Luce Press Clipping Service. See Bruce Buchanan, *Electing a President: The Markle Commission Research on Campaign '88* (Austin, TX: University of Texas Press, 1991), pp. 38–74. Based on all campaign news stories and editorials from thirteen major newspapers and NBC, ABC, CBS, CNN, and PBS. September 8–November 8, 1988. Some stories fit multiple categories.

[2]Conducted for the Markle Project by the Center for Media and Public Affairs. Based on all campaign news stories and editorials from the *New York Times, Washington Post, Wall Street Journal,* ABC, NBC, CBS, CNN, and PBS between September 7 and November 3, 1992. Some stories fit multiple categories.

[3]Conducted for the Markle Project by the Center for Media and Public Affairs. Based on all campaign news stories and editorials from ABC, CBS, and NBC between September 2 and November 4, 1996. Some stories fit multiple categories.

watched television networks that clarifies the policy differences between the candidates and by implication the likely policy consequences of particular voting choices. Differing campaign circumstances produce fluctuations in the cross-year patterns. But in general, we see that the preponderance of year-to-year coverage is devoted not to issues and qualifications but to competition and conflict. According to the Center for Media and Public Affairs (CMPA), the proportion of campaign stories about the campaign horse race—assessing each candidate's viability—reached 71 percent in 2000, a substantial increase over the three preceding elections.[31]

Economic incentives are behind these patterns just as surely as they are behind the reduction in coverage. The aim of holding the attention of the mass audience discourages policy coverage. That is why the focus of television coverage is on the novel, the colorful, the dramatic, and the conflictual. Fox TV news executive Roger Ailes aptly summed up the electronic media's prime coverage targets as: "pictures, polls, attacks, and mistakes."[32]

Reporters increasingly *interpret*, rather than merely describe, the horse race and other aspects of the campaign.[33] And interpretation means criticism. Not that critical coverage is out of bounds. The press in a free society is necessarily skeptical of the claims of power-seekers. That gives candidates reason to respect the truth and gives voters protection from disinformation. But the latest research suggests that useful skepticism is giving way to harmful exaggeration and cynicism. During the 1996 and 2000 presidential campaigns, for example, the major commercial television networks all but eliminated the most valuable form of candidate surveillance—"Ad

Watches" aimed at unmasking misleading or false political advertising, that debuted to wide acclaim in 1992.[34] Instead, critical coverage targeted campaign performance. In 1996, the net effect was to misrepresent what actually happened on the campaign trail. Coding shows that in 1996 the candidates offered three positive or self-promoting remarks for each criticism of a rival (74 percent positive). But the critical remarks made up a majority (52 percent) of the candidate quotes that made the evening news:

> Journalists painted a campaign portrait that was more negative than the reality; then they denounced the candidates' harsh tone. News coverage consisted mainly of criticism—of the presidential candidates, the parties, interest groups, campaign ads, and the electoral system itself."[35]

The net effect was to exaggerate the extent of the candidates' actual reliance on attack modes and to make the campaign seem more negative than it really was. Since the content and tone of television coverage influences the audience[36] the probable result was to encourage ill will toward the political process.

This likelihood is supported by a series of experiments that found that media coverage of campaigns and issues that highlights strategy and conflict activates political cynicism, defined as mistrust generalized from particular stories to the entire system.[37] As noted, conflict was overemphasized in 1996. And Patterson's[38] analysis of presidential campaign coverage from 1960 to 1992 shows that coverage has grown not only less substantive and more horse-race centered, but also more cynical. All of these findings support a conclusion that media coverage dwells on topics that alienate many potential voters.

Media Coverage Trivializes Policy   Research shows that issue coverage on network television tends to be quite superficial. A large coding study of 1996 presidential election coverage found that most references to candidate issue positions were short and insubstantial with little attention to the proposal's relation to the relevant national policy context, or to the proposal's potential policy implications, or to implications for voters' interests. For example, only 10 percent of 1996 post–Labor Day "issue mentions" were embedded in extensive and detailed policy stories that put issues in a larger context and also spelled out nonpolitical implications. The consequences for the election of candidates' records and proposals received the most attention, appearing in 43 percent of all issue discussions. This pattern held in 1992 as well as 1996, both years in which Table 1.1 shows that issue coverage was relatively high.[39] It probably also held in 1988, which the table shows to have featured much less media attention to policy, though comparable data are not available.

Such coverage tends to obscure the policy implications of candidate choices. If the goal were to help the mass audience get ready to vote, key details—like a list of the most important problems facing the nation, or the qualifications and issue positions of the candidates—would need to be repeated time and again, like commercial advertising. But repetition, however valuable it may be to voter learning, is out-of-bounds to journalists. "We're in the news business," they say, "and repetition of what has already been reported is not news." The well-established practice of not repeating already-reported information is obvious to any regular watcher of television news.

In sum, it is clear that media incentives result in coverage patterns that work against campaign quality. Reduced coverage limits both exposure to the campaign and to nonpartisan "free" media in comparison to paid ads, with obvious implications for voter interest, learning, and turnout. Minimal and trivial policy coverage limits the grasp the average citizen can achieve on the stakes of the election and the policy implications of candidate choice. Diminished candidate exposure means that reporters' spin—invariably stressing horse race and conflict rather than policy priorities and proposals—"frame" the campaign in ways that mislead the mass audience. And overcovering attack politics exaggerates the very feature of political practice—negativity—that discourages voting, even as it captures "train wreck" viewer attention helpful to the economic bottom line.

THE CITIZEN BALANCE SHEET

Citizens are the intended beneficiaries of representative democracy and the ultimate source of success—as measured by votes and ratings—for candidates and news organizations. Because of this, when voter-consumers make clear demands in numbers sufficient to threaten electoral or economic costs for noncompliance, candidates and journalists have little choice but to respond. On the other hand, signs of public indifference, such as low turnout, and ignorance of the policy stakes, invite self-serving campaign practice from the other actors. Given this tradeoff, citizens would seem to have good reason to stay involved. Instead, low turnout and policy ignorance predominate. Increasingly smaller percentages of eligible voters are willing to show up at the polls. And the public record of political learning is spotty at best, with Americans traditionally showing "minimal levels of political attention and information."[40] Many people have obviously concluded that participation is not worth the effort. The reason, as implied by the lists in Table 1.2, is that the disincentives to learn and vote are likely to outweigh the incentives for most potential voters in most presidential elections.

Incentives   Because it brings tens of millions of voters to the polls for every election, the most powerful and important citizen incentive is a socialized attitude: *civic duty*. Those who have internalized the charge to be

TABLE 1.2   VOTING AND LEARNING: CITIZEN INCENTIVES AND DISINCENTIVES

INCENTIVES	DISINCENTIVES
Civic duty	Divided government
Competitive election	Multiple elections
Policy anxiety	Workday voting
Political interest	No individual impact
Clear policy differences	High information cost
Policy impact	Registration cost
Party ID/loyalty	Alienation
	Indifference

dutiful see voting primarily as an obligation, to be sure, but also as a source of satisfaction.[41]

For most, civic duty begins and ends with voting. A November 1996 Princeton Survey Research Associates (PSRA) survey shows that while 70 percent of the electorate identifies voting as an important duty, only about 25 percent feels that way about learning (i.e., absorbing the information necessary to grasp the policy implications of the voting choice).

Usually, voters don't bother to learn very much about the problems facing the nation. But on the rare occasions when majorities do become better informed than usual, and make clear demands on the other actors, it is in response to one or another of the variable and unpredictable *situational* incentives in Table 1.2, especially policy anxiety.

It has long been known, for example, that turnout is highest when "issues of vital concern are presented,"[42] when elections are competitive, and when contesting candidates take clearly different policy stances.[43] Research on European electorates suggests that "electoral salience" (i.e., how much is at stake in terms of allocating government power) best explains turnout.[44] And such things as personal goals and interests, or the wish to help a candidate or promote a policy, will also increase the tendency to learn and vote among different people at different times.

Party label remains an important cue for most citizens, and party identifiers tend to be loyal supporters of their standard-bearers.[45] A Pew Research Center Poll released in November 1999 put self-described Republicans at 27, Democrats at 34 and Independents at 39 percent.[46] But the distribution of party identification is subject to change. Further, party ID is not a uniform incentive for all voters. Strong partisans of either party and all self-described Republicans continue to vote at very high levels (and are often inspired by the aggressive partisan tactics that turn others off). But weak partisans, Independents, and Democrats, who together make up nearly three-fourths of the voting age population, are low turnout groups.[47] And political Independents, the largest and fastest-growing group, are the most put off by attack politics.[48]

Voter Disincentives   That raises the specter of disincentives. Taken together, the disincentives to learn and vote are more powerful than the incentives for most citizens most of the time. The reason is that while many incentives are intermittent (e.g., policy anxiety, competitive elections), disincentives are more often structural and chronic, and thus more uniform in their influence from one election to the next. For example, 21 of the 39 presidential elections between 1840 and 1992 occurred during periods of divided government (i.e., a president of one party, a Congress of the other). And as Franklin and Hirczy de Mino[49] demonstrate, divided government and noncompetitive elections separately and significantly reduced voter turnout in American presidential elections between 1840 and 1992.

These and other researchers conclude that turnout declines because divided government and the separation of powers make the link between the vote and public policy ambiguous.[50] Apparently, a clear policy link draws voters by clarifying the stakes, while a fuzzy link slows turnout by confusing them.

Other equally demotivating circumstances are also imbedded fixtures of American political life. For example, U.S. voters face a daunting number of state, local, and federal voting opportunities. Even more discouraging is the fact that elections occur on workdays, which can impose financial as well as logistical barriers to participation. As if that were not enough, the U.S. registration barrier is said to reduce turnout by around 8 percent.[51] Add to this the not uncommon belief—widely shared most recently in 1996—that a particular election result is a foregone conclusion and the incentive to participate may dwindle even further.

Finally, those who believe that the most powerful incentive is self-interest think it is inoperative during elections because individual votes can't influence outcomes.[52] For candidates, elections are high cost, high reward events. By contrast, and the closeness of election 2000 notwithstanding, the benefits of voting are usually trivial for all but the dutiful. Since the costs are modest but not trivial, the incentive to vote is largely trumped. For systems beset with as many chronic disincentives as the United States, renewed efforts to inculcate sentiments like civic duty, expanded beyond just voting to include both learning and enforcement, would be worth making, a point I will revisit in Chapter 7.

Cumulative Effects   The long list of civic demotivators in Table 1.2 makes it clear that any alienation created by attack politics is far from the only explanation for nonparticipation. But when attacks are added to the structural disincentives, the widespread lack of intrinsic interest in matters political, and the universal awareness that one's vote counts for little, the alienation they engender may achieve something like "last straw" status. Why invest time, attention, and energy in an activity whose outcome does not affect you, whose content does not interest you, and whose bottom line you cannot affect, especially if you find the whole enterprise repugnant? From this angle, the decline in turnout makes sense, while the power of civic duty to mobilize voters by the millions seems even more impressive.

In sum, the mix of actor incentives shows why the typical campaign is most likely to be a low-quality rather than a high-quality event. In his examination of National Election Study (NES) 1952–1996 time-series data on public attitudes toward the electoral process, Bartels[53] notes that many of the benchmarks that made one campaign—1992—stand out as unusually successful, "saw the most dramatic reversion to long-term trend lines in 1996." As the standardizing power of incentives would lead us to predict, regression to the norm—declining political interest and diminished voter turnout—is the long-term trend.

CONCLUSION

Still, the occasional campaign does manage to beat the odds. The just-noted 1992 campaign is a case in point, and there are other policy-driven, high-interest elections scattered throughout American political history. The question is why, and the answer has precious little to do with the complaints of campaign critics. Politicians, reporters, and politically apathetic citizens have always seemed oblivious to campaign season exhortations to improve themselves in the name of good government. But what they cannot ignore are things that pose threats to the national well-being. External circumstances— the more ominous, the more powerful—can change how all the actors caught up in election campaigns understand their interests. Presidential contenders will always be driven to do what it takes to win. But the policy evasion and attacks that work in ordinary times (e.g., those confronting Bill Clinton in 1996 and George Bush in 1988) cannot work when the people are frightened or worried during a campaign season. Voters scared by the threat of nuclear war or by economic collapse will demand and get more of a focus on the problems that trouble them, as happened in both 1960 and 1992.

NOTES

1. Cf. Alan Gerber and Donald Green, "The Effects of Canvassing, Leafleting, and Direct Mail on Voter Turnout: A Field Experiment" (paper presented at the annual meeting of the Midwest Political Science Association, Chicago, IL, 1999); Steven J. Rosenstone and John Mark Hansen, *Mobilization, Participation, and Democracy in America* (New York: Macmillan, 1993).

2. Leslie Wayne, "A Lavish Run Leaves Forbes Laboring for Nation's Notice," *New York Times*, 31 December 1999, p. A-1.
3. S. Robert Lichter and Richard E. Noyes, *Good Intentions Make Bad News: Why Americans Hate Campaign Journalism*, 2nd ed. (Lanham, MD: Rowman and Littlefield, 1997).
4. Cf. Thomas E. Patterson, *Out of Order* (New York: Knopf, 1993); Joseph N. Capella and Kathleen Hall Jamieson, *Spiral of Cynicism: The Press and the Public Good* (New York: Oxford, 1997); S. Robert Lichter and Richard E. Noyes, *Good Intentions Make Bad News: Why Americans Hate Campaign Journalism*, 2nd ed. (Lanham, MD: Rowman and Littlefield, 1997).
5. Center for Media and Public Affairs, "Campaign '96: The Media and the Candidates," Final Report to the Markle Foundation (Washington, D.C.: 1998).
6. See, for example, Henry E. Brady, "A Review of the Markle Presidential Election Studies (unpublished manuscript, University of California, Berkeley, 1998); Robert C. Luskin, "Explaining Political Sophistication," *Political Behavior* 12 (1990), pp. 331–361; Angus Campbell, Philip E. Converse, Warren E. Miller, and Donald E. Stokes, *The American Voter* (Chicago: University of Chicago Press, 1960).
7. Bruce Buchanan, *Renewing Presidential Politics: Campaigns, Media, and the Public Interest* (Lanham, MD: Rowman and Littlefield, 1996).
8. David Broder, "Our Strangling Democracy," *Washington Post National Weekly Edition* (January 8–14, 1990), p. 4.
9. "Moral Authority," *Wall Street Journal*, 23 July 1998, p. A-16.
10. "The Smash-Mouth Presidency," *Wall Street Journal*, 13 August 1998, p. A-14.
11. Said longtime CBS News campaign reporter Bob Schieffer: ". . . [T]he press loves a good story. And the most recent good story in politics, the best story in politics in the last 40 years, was the McCain race. People talked about the positive coverage that John McCain got and asked, is it because the press loves John McCain? And my response always was, no, they love a great story, and this was a great story." Quoted in Bruce Buchanan, ed., *The State of the American Presidency* (Austin, TX: Lyndon Baines Johnson School of Public Affairs, 2002).
12. "Moral Authority," *Wall Street Journal*, 23 July 1998, p. A-16.
13. Bruce Buchanan, *Renewing Presidential Politics: Campaigns, Media, and the Public Interest* (Lanham, MD: Rowman and Littlefield, 1996).
14. Sidney Blumenthal, "The Ruins of Georgetown," *New Yorker*, 28 October 1996, p. 221.
15. Charles H. Franklin, "Eschewing Obfuscation? Campaigns and the Perceptions of U.S. Senate Incumbents," *American Political Science Review* 85 (1991), pp. 1193–1213.
16. Alan Murray, "Budget Gaps. The Fiscal Proposals of Bush and Clinton Both Flunk Arithmetic. Program Costs and Plans to Trim Taxes, Spending Leave Huge Shortfalls. Deficit Cuts That Aren't," *Wall Street Journal*, 15 September 1992, p. A-1.
17. John H. Aldrich, *Before the Convention: Strategies and Choices in Presidential Nomination Campaigns* (Chicago, IL: University of Chicago Press, 1980); Benjamin I. Page, *Choices and Echos in Presidential Elections* (Chicago, IL: University of Chicago Press, 1978); Anthony Downs, *An Economic Theory of Democracy* (New York: Harper & Row, 1957).
18. Dick Morris, *Behind the Oval Office* (New York: Random House, 1997).
19. Larry M. Bartels and Lynn Vavrek, eds., *Campaign Reform: Insights and Evidence* (Ann Arbor, MI: University of Michigan Press, 2000).
20. Dick Morris, *Behind the Oval Office* (New York: Random House, 1997), p. 138.
21. "Moral Authority," *Wall Street Journal*, 23 July 1998, p. A-16.
22. Dick Morris, *Behind the Oval Office* (New York: Random House, 1997), p. 145.
23. Richard A. Lau and Lee Sigelman, "The Effectiveness of Negative Political Advertising: A Literature Review" (paper presented at the American University Conference on Improving Campaign Conduct, Washington, D.C., April 1998).
24. Stephen Ansolabehere and Shanto Iyengar, *Going Negative: How Political Advertisements Shrink and Polarize the Electorate* (New York: Free Press, 1995); Robert C. Luskin and Christopher N. Bratcher, "Negative Campaigning, Partisanship, and Turnout" (paper presented at the annual meeting of the American Political Science Association, Chicago, 1995).
25. Steven E. Finkel and John G. Geer, "A Spot Check: Casting Doubt on the Demobilizing Effect of Attack Advertising," *American Journal of Political Science* 42 (1998), pp. 573–595.
26. Reginald K. Brack, Jr., "How to Clean up Gutter Politics," *New York Times*, 27 December 1994, p. A-15.

27. "2000 Year in Review," *Media Monitor* (January/February 2001), pp. 1–2 (Washington, D.C.: Center for Media and Public Affairs).
28. "Networks Skimped on Candidate, Issue Coverage during Campaign, Study Finds," *Political Standard* (Washington, D.C.: Alliance for Better Campaigns, December 2000), pp. 1–3.
29. Center for Media and Public Affairs, "Campaign '96: The Media and the Candidates," Final Report to the Markle Foundation (Washington, D.C.: 1998), p. 64; Thomas E. Patterson, *Out of Order* (New York: Knopf, 1993), pp. 75, 77.
30. "Networks Skimped on Candidate, Issue Coverage during Campaign, Study Finds," *Political Standard* (Washington, D.C.: Alliance for Better Campaigns, December 2000), pp. 1–3.
31. "2000 Year in Review," *Media Monitor* (January/February 2001), pp. 1–2 (Washington, D.C.: Center for Media and Public Affairs).
32. Larry McCarthy, "The Selling of the President: An Interview with Roger Ailes," *Gannett Center Journal* 2 (fall 1988): 65–72.
33. Thomas E. Patterson, *Out of Order* (New York: Knopf, 1993), p. 81.
34. Center for Media and Public Affairs, "Campaign '96: The Media and the Candidates," Final Report to the Markle Foundation (Washington, D.C.: 1998), p. 58.
35. Center for Media and Public Affairs, "Executive Summary," Final Report to the Markle Foundation (Washington, D.C.: 1998), pp. 5, 7.
36. Shanto Iyengar, *Is Anyone Responsible?* (Chicago, IL: University of Chicago Press, 1991); Shanto Iyengar and Donald Kinder, *News That Matters* (Chicago, IL: University of Chicago Press, 1987).
37. Joseph N. Cappella and Kathleen Hall Jamieson, *Spiral of Cynicism: The Press and the Public Good* (New York: Oxford, 1997), pp. 230–231.
38. Thomas E. Patterson, *Out of Order* (New York: Knopf, 1993).
39. Center for Media and Public Affairs, "Campaign '96: The Media and the Candidates," Final Report to the Markle Foundation (Washington, D.C.: 1998), pp. 36–41.
40. Paul M. Sniderman, "The New Look in Public Opinion Research," in *Political Science: The State of the Discipline II*, ed. Ada W. Finifter (Washington, D.C.: American Political Science Association, 1993), p. 219.
41. Morris P. Fiorina and Paul E. Peterson, *The New American Democracy* (Boston: Allyn and Bacon, 1998), p. 175.
42. Richard Boekel, *Voting and Non-Voting in Elections* (Washington, D.C.: Editorial Research Reports, 1928), p. 517; V. O. Key, *Politics, Parties, and Pressure Groups*, 5th ed. (New York: Crowell, 1964), p. 578.
43. Bernard Grofman, "Is Turnout the Paradox That Ate Rational Choice Theory?" in *Information, Participation, and Choice: An Economic Theory of Democracy in Perspective*, ed. Bernard Grofman (Ann Arbor: University of Michigan Press, 1993).
44. Cees van der Eijk and Mark Franklin, *Choosing Europe? The European Electorate and National Politics in the Face of Union* (Ann Arbor: University of Michigan, 1996); Karlheinz Reif and Hermann Schmitt, "Nine Second-Order National Elections: Conceptual Framework for the Analysis of European Election Results," *European Journal of Political Research* 8 (1980), pp. 3–44.
45. Norman R. Luttbeg and Michael M. Gant, *American Electoral Behavior, 1952–1992*, 2nd ed. (Itasca, IL: Peacock, 1995), p. 45.
46. "Retropolitics. The Political Typology: Version 3.0" (Washington, D.C.: Pew Research Center for the People and the Press, November 1999), p. 25.
47. Norman R. Luttbeg and Michael M. Gant, *American Electoral Behavior, 1952–1992*, 2nd ed. (Itasca, IL: Peacock, 1995), p. 110.
48. Stephen Ansolabehere and Shanto Iyengar, *Going Negative: How Political Advertisements Shrink and Polarize the Electorate* (New York: Free Press, 1995); Robert C. Luskin and Christopher N. Bratcher, "Negative Campaigning, Partisanship, and Turnout" (paper presented at the annual meeting of the American Political Science Association, Chicago, 1995).
49. Mark N. Franklin and Wolfgang P. Hirczy de Mino, "Separated Powers, Divided Government, and Turnout in U.S. Presidential Elections," *American Journal of Political Science* 42 (1998), pp. 316–326.
50. Cf. Herbert B. Asher, *Presidential Elections and American Politics: Voters, Candidates, and Campaigns since 1952* (Pacific Grove, CA: Brooks/Cole, 1992), p. 56; Nelson W. Polsby and Aaron Wildavsky, *Presidential Elections: Contemporary Strategies of American Electoral Politics* (New

York: Free Press, 1991), p. 331; Elmer E. Schattschneider, *The Semisovereign People: A Realist's View of Democracy in America* (New York: Holt, Rinehart and Winston, 1960), pp. 100–101.

51. Mark N. Franklin and Wolfgang P. Hirczy de Mino, "Separated Powers, Divided Government, and Turnout in U.S. Presidential Elections," *American Journal of Political Science* 42 (1998), pp. 316–326.

52. Anthony Downs, *An Economic Theory of Democracy* (New York: Harper & Row, 1957).

53. Larry Bartels, "Campaign Quality: Standards for Evaluation, Benchmarks for Reform" (paper presented at the annual meeting of the American Political Science Association, Washington, D.C., 1997), p. 47.

QUALITY FROM CRISIS

THE 1960 AND 1992 CAMPAIGNS

In every presidential election campaign since 1952, the National Election Studies survey (NES) of the University of Michigan has asked a random sample of citizens how interested they are in the ongoing campaign. The results show that the campaigns of 1960 and 1992 mark the high points in public interest. Further, much of the heightened interest in these campaigns was generated between Labor Day and Election Day, a distinct rarity for campaigns since 1952.[1]

Interest measures the urge to follow the campaign. It matters because strong interest is a telling precursor of the high-turnout, policy-centered election. Strong interest (plus such associated practices as discussing the campaign with others) is both the initial hook and a sustaining reason to follow the spectacle. The more interesting the campaign, the more likely are citizens to inform themselves, to clarify their expectations, and to vote. The higher the turnout and the clearer the policy expectations, the greater the likelihood that the president-elect, the Congress, and the media will perceive an election, even a close election, to have created popular pressure for important action.

The years 1960 and 1992 support these propositions. Both are high-quality campaigns. They illustrate the kinds of naturally occurring circumstances that mobilize voters and heighten their policy expectations. Though they differ in other ways, these two campaigns were both shaped at least in part by the anxieties of citizens, as well as by the attractions of novel and interesting candidates. These and other similarities, plus some of the differences, make the stories worth telling.

1960: THE COLD WAR

"The 1960 presidential contest," wrote Nixon biographer and British citizen Jonathan Aitken, "was the most exciting democratic election of the twentieth century."[2] This was only partly because of the issues before the country during the campaign. In fact, one influential observer, journalist and campaign chronicler Theodore H. White, felt that the campaign was not particularly enlightening: "Rarely in American history has there been a political campaign that discussed the issues less or clarified them less." That conclusion, a product of its time, reflects a misunderstanding of how issues actually draw energy and momentum from campaigns. Too, far less substantive campaigns than seemed typical in 1960—1984 and 1988 are good examples—lay ahead. But it is undeniable that attention often focused on things other than issues in 1960, especially personalities.

The youthful, good-looking, and wealthy Democratic candidate, Massachusetts senator John F. Kennedy, whose handicaps included his Catholic religion and his lack of experience, was up against the slightly older but much more experienced Republican vice president, Richard M. Nixon, whose disadvantages were his reputation for "below-the-belt" politics and his need to defend the record of the Eisenhower administration before a mass public jury dominated by registered Democrats.

Both men were extraordinarily gifted politicians, impressive speakers, and conceptual thinkers with little time to expound ideas in the midst of a heated political campaign. And both were energetic and determined competitors, willing to go the extra mile to win. Nixon, for example, promised to campaign in all fifty states. Kennedy was scarcely less frenetic, driving himself to the point of exhaustion in the closing days of what turned out to be the closest election to that point in American history.

The public fascination with this campaign was obviously driven in part by attractive leading characters. But Kennedy's aggressive campaign strategy—an attack on the complacency of the Eisenhower administration—was also a factor. Kennedy's persistent emphasis on "getting the country moving again," together with his rhetorical habit of challenging the American people directly ("The New Frontier of which I speak is not a set of promises. It is a set of challenges.") seemed to energize his audiences. His star quality was enhanced by his assertiveness. "More and more, Kennedy's charisma stirred Americans, as he polished the cadence of his speeches, delivered with a crisp Boston accent and a finger repeatedly thrust forward to emphasize a point."[3]

Kennedy's appeal was showcased by an historic series of televised debates viewed by what was then the largest campaign audience in American history. Some 80 million people watched the first encounter, with the audiences for the three remaining debates pegged at around 60 million.[4] Kennedy aide Theodore Sorensen called the debates "a primary reason for the increasing interest in the campaign and the record turnout at the polls."[5] Finally, the campaign was all the more compelling for being a cliffhanger. Virtually every Gallup and Roper poll taken between January and August 1960 showed a close race; those taken between the debates and Election Day showed Nixon and Kennedy running neck and neck.

If little of the excitement of the 1960 campaign can be attributed to the debate over policy, it is at least in part because the candidates did not disagree profoundly on the major questions of the day. Both accepted the welfare state at home and the doctrine of containing the Soviet Union abroad. And both party platforms had civil rights planks that each candidate endorsed. In fact, Nixon had been instrumental in crafting ". . . the most liberal platform on civil rights ever to be accepted by the Republican Party."[6]

"I subscribe completely to the spirit that Senator Kennedy has expressed tonight," said Nixon during the first debate on September 26. "The goals are the same for all Americans," agreed Kennedy. "[Only] the means are at question."[7] There were differences on matters of economic policy, and on government programs versus private enterprise. There were also differences of tone and emphasis. But it is entirely likely that a postelection policy agenda dominated by Soviet relations, economic growth, and civil rights would have characterized a Nixon administration just as it came to dominate Kennedy's.

It is not surprising, then, that the most controversial questions of the 1960 campaign did not concern high policy. Attention to the great questions ebbed and flowed with events, sometimes coming to the fore, but often relegated to the background. Instead, the most heated dispute was over the significance of Kennedy's religious affiliation as a Catholic, a question that did more to excite voters than foreign policy, though few would have denied that the Soviet challenge was of far greater importance to the country. Kennedy adviser Theodore Sorensen cites pollsters who said that more people spoke passionately of Kennedy's religion than of any other factor in the campaign.[8]

Views of the impact of Kennedy's religion are partisan. Those who said it helped Kennedy included Nixon himself and, more recently, conservative historian Paul Johnson.[9] Those who said it hurt him were democrats.[10] In any case, the issue gave Kennedy a chance, in a September 12 television address to the Ministerial Association of Houston, to attract attention and show poise under fire.

Still, the major policy consequences of this election did not concern the greater future access to the presidency of Catholic candidates (no Catholic has been elected since 1960). They did not even concern such high-profile Kennedy legacies as the Peace Corps, the only brand-new proposal Kennedy put on the table during the campaign[11] and an innovation that endures to this day. In other words, the things that did the most to stir passion and excitement during the campaign—religion, glamour, high-stakes debates, a cliffhanger of a race—were ultimately not the things that did the most to shape important policy. Neither, arguably, was the identity of the victor, despite the fact that Kennedy himself would become a fixture of American political culture in the decades following his assassination.

Instead, the major consequences of the election would involve peace, prosperity, and civil rights. These issues were known to be important, were frequently and sometimes intensively discussed by the candidates (especially the Soviet threat), and were identified as high priorities by voters, despite not always being at the center of attention. As we see next, public expectations and government policy in all three areas would be significantly influenced, though in very different ways, by forces both deliberately and accidentally unleashed during the campaign.

EXPECTATION: MEET THE SOVIET THREAT

What put questions of peace and war at the top of the campaign agenda? Widespread public anxiety over the Cold War competition with the Soviet Union, a competition heightened in 1959 and 1960 by a worsening of Soviet–U.S. relations. That is what led both Kennedy and Nixon to feature, throughout the contest, their plans for bettering America's strength and stature in the world. And that is what led Kennedy to strike his famously aggressive inaugural pose (". . . we will pay any price, bear any burden . . .") toward the Soviets. The Soviet threat was the dominant issue of the campaign and a continuing source of mass anxiety.

The larger impetus for the public's cold war anxiety during the 1960 presidential contest was the successful October 4, 1957, launching by the Soviet Union of *Sputnik*, the world's first orbiting satellite. This dramatic accomplishment created the impression that the Soviets had outpaced the United States in rocketry. Soviet Premier Nikita Khrushchev's bombastic visit to the U.S. in September 1959, best remembered for his use of a shoe as a gavel during a United Nations address, and for his boast that "We will bury you," added to the sense of foreboding. Democratic politicians began assailing the Eisenhower administration for failing to keep pace with the enemy. Charges of a "missile gap" would be flung at the GOP during both the 1958 and 1960 election campaigns. Both President Eisenhower and Vice President Nixon knew that there was no missile gap; that the United States had a huge advantage over the Soviets in military missile development and in nuclear weaponry. In fact, the Soviets lagged badly in the production of usable warheads and intercontinental ballistic missiles (ICBMs). But the Eisenhower administration could not reveal this information without disclosing its U-2 reconnaissance plane spy program. That, Eisenhower feared, would worsen Soviet–American relations (which did happen when the Soviets finally shot down a U-2 spy plane in May 1960) and could push the Soviet leadership into a massive military buildup. The "missile gap" charge unanswered, critics began to speak of "a lack of national purpose" under Republican leadership.[12]

The intensifying cold war represented a target of opportunity for the Democratic challenger. In the first debate with Nixon, Kennedy framed the issue: "The question before us all—the question that faces all Democrats and all Republicans—is, can freedom in the next generation conquer, or will the communists be successful—that's the great issue. . . ." He went on the attack, hammering both the missile gap and the lack of national purpose, pledging, as noted, to "get the country moving again." As he had in the January 1960 speech announcing his candidacy, as he did in the debates, and as he would later in his inaugural address, he called for sacrifice: "The New Frontier is here whether we seek it or not—in uncharted areas of science and space, unsolved problems of peace and war, unconquered pockets of ignorance and prejudice, unanswered questions of poverty and surplus."[13]

Nixon, whose major theme was his long experience in national government and foreign policy, would be forced to defend the policies of the Eisenhower administration. "I said that, far from standing still, the nation had experienced eight years of its greatest progress in history under Eisenhower, largely because of his sound policies."[14] But he echoed Kennedy's identification of ". . . the one great issue of the campaign: how to keep the peace without surrender of territory or principle, and how to preserve and extend freedom everywhere in the world."[15]

Kennedy was able to attack Eisenhower's failure to keep pace with the Soviet Union in education and technology, as well as ICBMs. He blamed the Eisenhower-Nixon administration for America's declining prestige in the world, especially among newly emerging nations in Africa and Asia, the key new battlegrounds of the Cold War. He also pointed to the loss of Cuba to the Communists and the failure of the summit conference after the disastrous U-2 affair in May.[16] The U-2 crisis dashed hopes of an evolving detente and plunged the Cold War back into freeze mode, where it remained through the election and beyond.

EVIDENCE OF PUBLIC ANXIETY

Asked by Gallup Poll interviewers in February which country was further ahead in missiles and rockets, respondents chose Russia over the United States by 47 to 33 percent. But nothing revealed the intensely personal nature of the public's Cold War anxiety at this perception of Russian superiority better than a Gallup Poll published on June 3 showing that 71 percent of a national sample favored a law requiring each community in the United States to build public bomb shelters.[17] An earlier Gallup Poll, published on March 2, had reported that an overwhelming majority named issues dealing with foreign policy as "the most important problem facing the country today." Relatedly, a telephone survey of 1,200 voters taken August 13–18 yielded the rank-ordering of the public's issue priorities depicted in Table 2.1 on page 26.[18]

The first three priorities identified in the table deal with the emotional pushes and pulls of the effort to negotiate with a formidable adversary from a position of strength. All the rest deal with the other two major policy priorities at stake in the election: civil rights (with states rights as the rallying cry of those opposed to increasing protections for the civil rights of black citizens) and economic concerns.

TABLE 2.1   VOTER ISSUE PRIORITIES, AUGUST 1960

Negotiating with the Russians
Keeping ahead of the Russians
Developing missiles
Keeping prices down
Civil rights
Old folks
Employment
States rights
Farm income

Source: Ithiel de Sola Pool, Robert P. Abelson, and Samuel L. Popkin, *Candidates, Issues, and Strategies: A Computer Simulation of the 1960 and 1964 Presidential Elections* (Cambridge, MA: The M.I.T. Press, 1964), p. 86.

Despite the greater attention paid to such questions as Kennedy's religion, then, and even though postelection polls would show that other issues had increased in importance (A January 1961 Gallup poll,[19] asking what the new president and Congress should emphasize, had economic concerns in the first four places, civil rights in fifth, and the Soviet threat all the way down to sixth place.), it was still very clear that President-elect Kennedy was expected, in the words of the survey, to "find a new and different way to handle problems with Russia." Since a young and aggressive new president of a party out of power for eight long years had been elected to do just that, Americans could shift some attention to the economic issues the new president had emphasized on the campaign trail.

PROMISE: INCREASE ECONOMIC GROWTH AND JUSTICE

The Soviet challenge was the central issue facing the country during the 1960 campaign, not because the candidates made it so, but because clear and widespread public anxiety forced it to the top of the agenda. Economic issues, on the other hand, became a priority not because of preexisting and widespread public demand (there was no economic crisis such as FDR had faced in 1932) but because candidate Kennedy succeeded in persuading many Americans that certain economic conditions—moderately increasing unemployment, a 3 percent growth rate the candidate portrayed as sluggish, and increasingly visible poverty—showed a need for a change in policy.

One columnist summarized Kennedy's indictment tersely: "The American economy is stagnating: We are falling behind the Soviet Union and behind the leading industrial nations of Western Europe in our rate of growth."[20] Thus, the domestic side of Kennedy's pledge to "get America moving again" had a heavy economic as well as a foreign policy component.

Many of the programs for achieving the economic goals Kennedy raised near the top of the national agenda would not be devised until after the election.[21] Notable actions taken during Kennedy's presidency, such as the "big tax cut that is still remembered as the great triumph of Kennedy economics"[22] were not discussed during the campaign. The specific proposals that were discussed were drawn largely from the scripts of the Democratic and Republican Party platforms. The Democratic plan included a jobs program, area redevelopment to deal with structural unemployment, especially in the hard-hit farming sector of the economy, concern for the poor, aid to education, and Medicare for the aged. In his speeches, Kennedy stressed unemployment in depressed areas, low wages and the minimum wage, federal aid to education, medical care for the aged, and the eradication of urban blight.[23] Most often, however, Kennedy's economic rhetoric hammered problems, not solutions: the slow rate of economic growth, neglect of the poor and aged ("17 million Americans go to bed hungry at night"), and the economic plight of the farmer, which he called "our number one domestic problem." The implicit message was that new government spending programs would be established to address these problems. The Republican platform called for policies and programs that gave incentives to the free enterprise system to accelerate economic growth. It featured price support programs to enhance farm income and more rapid disposal of the crop surpluses that depressed agricultural profits.[24] Also included were a contributory system for the elderly to purchase health insurance, a revision of the minimum wage, and action to improve manpower training.[25]

Aware of his vulnerability to an opponent willing to offer more substantial new benefits to those in trouble, Nixon had sought unsuccessfully to get Eisenhower to work to loosen credit and to increase defense spending early enough to generate good economic news during the campaign that could neutralize the economy as a political issue.[26] Without good news to trumpet, Nixon was at a competitive disadvantage. He could only chide Kennedy for fiscal irresponsibility: "I pointed out that Kennedy was a 'Pied Piper,' saying 'give me your money and I will solve all your problems.' I struck hard at his 'switch-hit' tactics: He was a 'jumping Jack' who promised vast new spending programs but no new taxes and no deficits. . . ."[27] The Nixon counterattack on economic policy, as summed up by Theodore H. White, was that "the Democratic platform, if put into effect, would raise the price of everything the housewife buys by 25 percent."[28]

Kennedy knew that many of his spending proposals would face tough sledding in a Congress dominated by conservative Southern Democrats. But during the campaign, his economic goals were framed like the foreign policy goals: as part of the larger effort to best the Soviets, and in the process to reinvigorate a nation grown sluggish under the grandfatherly Eisenhower.[29] In the end, public support for economic revitalization was indeed mobilized. But again, it was a byproduct of the Kennedy campaign, not of preexisting and widespread economic anxiety. It shows the ability of a candidate with a plausible argument to put an issue on the public's agenda. Kennedy himself created the expectations—full employment, more rapid growth, a reduction in poverty and an increase in the quality of life—he would have to meet as president.

MORAL IMPERATIVE: PROMOTE RACIAL JUSTICE

The third of the big issues showcased by the 1960 campaign—civil rights—was neither a candidate initiative nor a strong public demand. Indeed, it was not a big issue at all during most of the campaign for any but the civil rights activists clamoring to stir the national conscience. Though neither candidate emphasized the issue on the stump for fear of alienating Southern votes, both the Democratic and the Republican platforms had liberal civil rights planks. Stung by the Democratic sweep of Congress in 1958, the Republican platform of 1960 moved to the center by featuring such usually Democratic issues as civil rights, voting, desegregation, housing, schools, and jobs.

For his part, Kennedy was as eager as Nixon to avoid the politically explosive question of civil rights. But the issue got an unexpected boost when, late in the campaign, Martin Luther King, Jr., was arrested for leading a group of protesters into a whites-only restaurant and demanding service. King was jailed following a lunch-counter sit-in, provoking fear that he might be lynched in jail. At this point, both candidates faced the question of whether to confront the issue publicly. Nixon demurred, but Kennedy responded to staff pressure and his own instincts to telephone Mrs. King and offer to intervene if necessary. Later, Kennedy's brother, Bobby, the future Attorney General, called a Federal judge who arranged for King's release from jail. Mrs. King told her friends and the news spread through the African-American community to the press. Nixon suffered and Kennedy gained at the polls as a result of these events, as the black community rallied behind Kennedy, helping him to his razor-thin margin of victory.

Although the general public considered the civil rights issue to be an important one, its fifth place ranking in the Pool et al. summer poll (Table 2.1) had not changed by the January 1961 Gallup poll cited earlier. Thus, two Kennedy family phone calls on behalf of Martin Luther King, Jr., did not do as much to raise the priority of this issue in the public mind as the Kennedy economic policy rhetoric did to raise the profile of economic issues (which moved, as noted earlier, into the top four places by December of 1961). Still, the phone calls had consequences that would influence postelection policy toward civil rights.

First, they publicly and dramatically linked Kennedy to an issue from which he had previously tried to distance himself. Second, his action emboldened the civil rights leadership to press an elected Kennedy that much harder, both to keep the civil rights promises in the Democratic platform, and to lend his prestige to the cause as president as he had as a candidate. Sorensen, with both the campaign gesture and postelection Kennedy actions in mind, observes: ". . . [T]he sympathy (Kennedy) displayed, the appointees he assembled, the courage he demonstrated in placing himself at the head of that revolution, all encouraged a climate for reform and a reason for hope within the Southern Negro leadership. Their new efforts and pressures would probably not have been risked had there been a much different attitude in the White House and in the Department of Justice."[30] And third, although Kennedy was personally inclined to be supportive, his sense of political obligation to press a civil rights agenda was strengthened by the fact that Northern black votes (much of the black population in the South was effectively disenfranchised) had helped him to his narrow election victory. To be sure, later events—the Freedom Rides of 1961, the forced integration of James Meredith into the University of Mississippi in 1962, the 1963 Birmingham, Alabama, crisis that put Bull Connor and his police dogs on national television—put more direct pressure on Kennedy the president to act than did two 1960 campaign phone calls. But by helping to put civil rights near the top of a new president's agenda, those unplanned campaign events set in motion the forces that eventually led Kennedy to deliver, on June 11, 1963, the strongest presidential address on civil rights in American history, and in the same month to propose a legislative measure that eventually became the Civil Rights Act of 1964.

MEDIA: PAID AND UNPAID

What role did journalism and paid advertising play in focusing the 1960 campaign on policy? A mixed but largely positive one. Kennedy successfully cultivated media attention for years in preparation for seeking the presidency. A systematic program of publicity emphasizing his largely staff-authored books and articles, his status as the Pulitzer-prize winning author of *Profiles in Courage*, and as a war hero, helped to put him at the head of the Democratic pack for the 1960 nomination.[31] Once the campaign was underway Kennedy used paid advertising to publicize and exploit his World War II heroics. A half-hour documentary was aired in the Wisconsin primary, followed by a five-minute general election ad focused on Kennedy's heroism and physical vigor in rescuing his crew when the Japanese sank PT-109. Later investigation disclosed that Kennedy suffered from Addison's disease, which he treated with mood-altering cortical steroids. The trumpeting of the PT-109 incident was intended in part to inoculate Kennedy against questions about whether his condition and its treatment should disqualify him from serving as president.[32] The strategy was deceptive, but it worked. Similarly, the "missile gap," used effectively by Kennedy as a campaign weapon against Nixon, was later shown to be without basis in fact, although Sorensen and other Kennedy intimates defended the propriety of the charge.[33]

Apart from these misrepresentations on Kennedy's part, both he and Nixon generally focused their media and traveling campaigns on major issues and their respective policy proposals.[34] The result was that both candidate advertising and media campaign coverage were much more issue-based in 1960 than would become the norm in later presidential campaigns. Jamieson[35] reports that ads were lengthy (modal time: five minutes, compared to thirty seconds or less in most ads used in the 1990s) and 75 percent substantive. She also reports that in addition to their regular newscasts, the networks devoted over forty-one hours to campaign programs, many of which synopsized candidate issue arguments and called attention to candidate exaggerations and distortions of fact. Further, "the reporting conventions of 1960 dictated that every major speech by a candidate be summarized." Jamieson concludes that despite the "fake missile gap and . . . fictions about Kennedy's health, the 1960 Kennedy-Nixon campaign produced the most robust, engaged, accountable discourse of any in the history of television."

1960 CAMPAIGN CONSEQUENCES

Neither the analysts nor the president-elect himself saw a policy mandate for Kennedy in his razor-thin victory over Nixon.[36] Such a conclusion was superficially true. But it overlooked the clear policy signal that began with alarmed voters, gathered steam with such campaign salvos as the missile gap charge, and was confirmed by the election as the new president's top priority. The depth of public concern made it likely that the president-elect, whoever he was and however small his margin of victory turned out to be, would have as his first priority a strengthening of America's competitive position in the world. That mood contributed to a variety of specific postelection policy consequences, ranging from increases in defense spending and expenditures for space exploration to an intensified arms and technology race to support for anticommunist movements around the globe to a perilous confrontation with the Soviets over nuclear missiles in Cuba.

1992: THE PHANTOM RECESSION

The economic indicators were improving as Election Day, 1992, approached. But the news had not pierced the awareness of most voters:

> Voters still bought into the Clinton campaign's cry that "the economy, stupid," was everyone's problem. It made GOP strategist Charlie Black want to tear out his hair. "I can't tell you why this happens, but there's a lag time" before people tune in to good economic news, he says.[37]

Economic Anxiety

The slow recognition of an improving economy—seven weeks after election day 1992, economists announced that the recession had ended in March 1991—was one reason why the voters' concerns about the economy could set the tone of the campaign.[38] The man who lost the election, former president George Bush, blamed the media for not spreading the word:

> When near the end of my term I said the economy was recovering the [media] stated, all but unanimously, that I was out of touch. The economy had indeed recovered. We handed Pres. Clinton a fast growing economy but none of the fall reporting that I recall credited us with any of this recovery.[39]

The people simply did not believe there was a recovery. By the fall of 1991, Bush's own internal polling found 80 percent of the public still agreeing that "the country is in a recession right now."[40] By November of 1991, the public had grown even more pessimistic. A Wall Street Journal/NBC News poll showed that "32 percent of voters think the economy will get worse in the next year, while only 26 percent think it will get better," an almost exact reversal of the "better-worse" percentages from the previous month.[41]

The President Responds

Bush was mindful of growing bipartisan criticism that his administration was failing to address the nation's economic ills. He knew that many inside the Republican Party believed he was endangering his own chances of reelection by ignoring the widespread perception that the economy still faced significant problems. Bush's response was to call a press conference on November 18, 1991, to make a public announcement that he would do—nothing. He said that neither he nor most top economists believed that the nation would slide back into recession in 1992:

> You see, there's some fairly good fundamentals getting out there . . . inflation is down. Interest rates are down. Personal debt is down . . . exports are up. So it's not like we're dealing with a totally bad economy. . . . No radically different approaches [are needed].[42]

The president went on to say that his existing legislative program, which included proposals to cut the capital gains tax rate, an overhaul of the banking system and a highway bill that would create jobs, were more than sufficient, if Congress would only pass them. He concluded that his immediate problem was largely one of public relations. "I think I've got to do better making clear what the message is."[43]

BUSH VULNERABILITIES

By June of 1992, with polls showing that 78 percent of registered voters dis-approved of his economic performance, Bush was still resisting political ad-vice that his reelection depended on convincing the public that he would take decisive action to stimulate economic growth. Instead, he confined him-self to "jawboning" the Federal Reserve for easier credit.[44] Press accounts and polls make it clear that the net effect of Bush pronouncements on the economy in the twelve months preceding the 1992 election—whose content and tone is well-represented by the press encounter of November 1991 ex-cerpted earlier—was to reinforce the impression that he was "doing noth-ing" in the face of what many Americans saw as a crisis because he had no coherent economic plan.

The political damage done by Bush's refusal to take even symbolic eco-nomic policy action was magnified by the second of his political vulnerabili-ties: his patrician image, which made him an easy target for those who sought to portray him as insensitive to the plight of working families anxious about their jobs and the economy. The most frequently repeated illustration of Bush's alleged insensitivity was the "supermarket scanner" story.

Prior to a speech before the National Grocers' Association in 1992, Bush was shown a display of a scanner that used newfangled technology. "Isn't that something," he said. *New York Times* reporter Andrew Rosenthal put the episode into a story that portrayed Bush as "so out-of-touch that he'd never seen a grocery checkout scanner before." An irritated Bush told his press sec-retary, Marlin Fitzwater, that it was brand new technology, not the familiar checkout scanner technology, that had prompted his remark. Though a few re-porters later corrected the story, the damage was done. The Rosenthal por-trayal became the standard interpretation. Said Fitzwater in his memoirs: "It was a classic and sums up the frustration we all felt about a story that essen-tially was manufactured and against which we had little recourse."[45]

The public view of Bush as out-of-touch with ordinary people was ce-mented late in the campaign by Bush's seeming inability to grasp the con-cerns of Marisa Hall, who during the October 19 candidate debate before a group of voters at the University of Richmond in Virginia, asked the candi-dates: "How has the national debt personally affected each of your lives? And if it hasn't, how can you honestly find a cure for the economic problems of the common people if you have no experience in what's ailing them?" Said Bush, after two halting and abortive attempts to respond: "I'm not sure I get—help me with the question and I'll try to answer it." Marisa Hall later underscored Bush's empathy deficit with the public: "President Bush never answered it. It kind of upset me."[46]

Finally, George Bush's participation in the 1990 budget agreement alien-ated a large portion of his own party, which further increased his vulnerabil-ity. The budget agreement was a Bush initiative, taken to stem the growth of the budget deficit that he and Dukakis had ignored in the '88 campaign. The agreement made the president complicit with Democrats in a tax increase that economic conservatives believed had contributed to the sluggish economy.[47] To House Republican majority leader Richard Armey of Texas, "no betrayal seems greater" than the Bush capitulation to the Democrats on taxes. "The [budget deal] drove a wedge between the president and fellow Republicans going into the 1992 elections."[48] Pat Buchanan, the conservative television commentator-turned-presidential-candidate who would challenge and damage Bush politically in the Republican primaries, linked his decision to run to the budget agreement of 1990. "Like a lot of conservatives," said Buchanan, "I felt he'd broken the main commitment he'd made for us."[49] The budget agreement insured that unhappiness with Bush's economic performance would cut across party lines.

Unhappiness with the incumbent's response to economic distress was decisive in making a serious economics debate likely during the 1992 campaign. But it was not the only important factor. There was also an interplay among several other events and circumstances, each of which eventually contributed to a better-than-average policy discussion and a jump in turnout.

MULTIPLE, IMPROBABLE CANDIDATES

The first such circumstance was that the candidate field, which emerged before the economy became a major public concern, was shaped by a premature conclusion that the incumbent was unbeatable. President Bush reached 88 percent approval in the CBS News/New York Times poll taken in March 1991 at the close of the Gulf War.[50] That discouraged leading Democratic Party politicians such as New York governor Mario Cuomo, Tennessee Senator Al Gore, and House Majority Leader Richard Gephardt from challenging Bush's bid for a second term. The absence of the "first string" encouraged less well-known Democrats, such as Governor Bill Clinton of Arkansas, to step forward. And together with the antipolitics backlash discussed next, it also drew several long-shot contenders, including Paul Tsongas and Ross Perot, into the race.

POLITICAL BACKLASH

Second, intense public displeasure with campaign '88 had made the health of the political system and the public's discontent with attack politics a recurring object of media attention. This, in turn, made the bankruptcy of traditional politics a frequent subject of discussion. And it made the political strategies of candidates the object of intense scrutiny. These circumstances inspired both regional and national media to embark on a program of truth testing candidate claims. Together with the antipolitical mood of the country, the scrutiny would help to prevent a repeat of the highly successful attack-ad-centered strategy of the 1988 Bush campaign.

ADVERTISING RECONFIGURED

This is not to suggest that political advertising was eliminated. By some accounts, it remained quite influential. But it was redesigned. And with one important exception, it was relegated to a much lower profile than it had enjoyed in 1988. Clinton's winning ad strategy, for example, was to avoid national advertising altogether, investing heavily instead in local ads limited to twenty key states. Also avoided were what Clinton ad team representative Mandy Grunwald described as "bitchy negative ads" in favor of what Clinton termed "fact-slinging, not mudslinging."[51]

An unexpected development was the fact that the attack ads that *were* used in 1992 showed that they could produce unintended effects in what became a three candidate race. The Bush camp attacked Ross Perot in June, for example, and succeeded in raising his negatives in the minds of many voters. But unexpectedly, it was Clinton, not Bush, who benefited from Perot's decline. That led the Clinton camp to resist the temptation to attack Perot themselves. And it led Bush handlers to avoid attacks on Clinton until the desperate late stages of the campaign.[52] It is probable that the reduced incidence of aggressive attack advertising played some part in the higher levels of satisfaction with the campaign reported by voters after the election.[53]

The exception to this low-profile approach turned into the most noticed and most popular advertising campaign of 1992. It consisted of informal fifteen-to thirty-minute "infomercials" in which Texas billionaire and political maverick Ross Perot used graphs and charts to explain the budget deficit and other complex policy issues. It is likely that Perot's infomercials helped to increase both citizen interest and media attention to the budget deficit and the economy. A citizen relying on television news for a sense of the 1992 campaign was likely to conclude that, compared to 1988, political ads were not only less frequent and less mean-spirited, but also more truthful, interesting and informative, especially when Perot was involved.

TSONGAS AND PEROT

The most important consequence of the antipolitics backlash was the emergence of self-consciously nontraditional candidates like former California governor Jerry Brown, former Massachusetts Senator Paul Tsongas, and Ross Perot. All three sought to deploy less self-serving and more substantive campaigns. And two—Tsongas and Perot—took action that intensified the influence of voter economic anxiety on the campaigns of the eventual major party nominees.

Paul Tsongas was the first to act, converting anti-Bush economic anxiety into a movement that would outlast his own candidacy. Tsongas inspired

Ross Perot, and though they acted separately, together they would turn the campaign into a referendum on the future of national economic policy. Tsongas set the tone for the campaign year with his determination to be a "Johnny-one-note" on the economy, his message that there could be no true economic revival without a strong manufacturing base, and his publication and promotion of an eighty six-page issue booklet entitled *A Call to Economic Arms*. Perot and other candidates, including Democrats Tom Harkin and Bill Clinton as well as incumbent George Bush would all eventually produce their own booklet-length policy plans, making 1992 the "year of the booklet" in presidential politics.[54]

Tsongas, who was the first Democrat to declare his candidacy, did so at a time, April 1991, when George Bush still looked unbeatable. He was moved to attempt a seemingly hopeless presidential run by his need to "give something back" in return for his survival of a bout with cancer.[55] He took Bush's 1991 State of the Union comment that "we were the most productive nation on earth," as evidence that Bush would not "use his enormous political capital to deal with the realities that all of us saw out in the private sector."[56] His campaign was an effort to force the political debate to confront the sort of painful economic realities and choices usually avoided by mainstream candidates pressing self-serving and opportunistic campaigns.

Tsongas managed to parlay his no-nonsense economic message—encapsulated in his signature line, "I'm not Santa Claus"—into a victory over Bill Clinton in the Democratic primary in New Hampshire, where economic conditions were among the worst in the nation. More than any other events, the Tsongas New Hampshire campaign and victory established the perception—shared from that time forward by media and the other candidates—that the voters were mobilized to demand a serious campaign focused on the economy. Ross Perot reinforced that message—and ensured that major party nominees Bush and Clinton knew it would be enforced at the polls—with an historically important "outsider" campaign that further intensified the public's demand for deficit reduction and economic growth. Perot acted to mobilize voters in several specific ways.[57] From his initial (February 20) appearance on *Larry King Live*, to his explosive ascent to the top spot in the polls in June (the only outsider candidate ever to achieve first place), to his quixotic departure from the race on July 17, to his reentry on October 1, to his winning debate performances, to his infomercials and pronouncements stressing his signature issue, the budget deficit, and the inadequacies of traditional politics and parties, Perot drew national public attention to the campaign as did no other actor or event. He further entrenched the policy focus initiated by Tsongas, forced the other candidates to address it more specifically than they would otherwise have done, and discouraged the use of attack advertising in ways already suggested. Both individually and in conjunction with Tsongas and the voters both men mobilized, Perot was instrumental in generating the clearest campaign policy signal since the Reagan campaign of 1980, and in attracting the largest voter turnout since the 1960 presidential campaign.

1992 CAMPAIGN CONSEQUENCES

There were many well-publicized detours into character questions, raised mostly by Clinton's Gennifer Flowers, marijuana, and draft evasion troubles. And despite Perot's pressure, the major party candidates still evaded and overpromised, as implied by the headline of one particularly effective example of watchdog journalism in the *Wall Street Journal* that Perot himself frequently cited: "The Fiscal Proposals of Bush and Clinton Both Flunk Arithmetic."[58] Nevertheless, it was clear that 1992 was different. The comparative data in Chapter 5 (Table 5.2, page 84) show that the post–Labor Day 1992 race was more of an issues campaign than either 1988 or 1996, and focused mainly on candidate proposals for fixing the economy. Grades given by voters to candidates, media, and themselves in 1988, 1992, and 1996 in Pew Research Center Polls were highest in 1992, as was overall satisfaction with the campaign.[59]

Ultimately, it was voter demand—sparked by economic anxiety and focused by Tsongas and Perot—that forced a more substantive, positive, and participative campaign in 1992. By their response to pollsters, their primary votes, and their reactions to highly unusual outsider candidates, voters made it clear to the major party nominees that a different approach was needed. As New York Times reporter Robin Toner put it at campaign's end, "This was a big, sweeping, utterly serious campaign that left little in its path unchanged. . . . From the New Hampshire primary on, the voters provided a merciless reality check on the candidates; those who strayed from the economy for very long were quickly punished."[60]

CONCLUSION

The contests between John F. Kennedy and Richard M. Nixon in 1960 and between Bill Clinton, George Herbert Walker Bush, and Ross Perot in 1992, though quite different in many respects, had two important things in common. Each featured a substantive policy debate about the best way to address the nation's number-one problem. And each policy discussion attracted record interest followed by levels of turnout—nearly 63 percent in 1960 and 55 percent in 1992—that were big improvements in context. The atypical focus on top national priorities and the jumps in turnout happened because Americans felt threats to their peace and prosperity and turned to the political process *en masse* for answers. The press of their anxieties drove candidates and news organizations to respond with the sort of campaign performances that campaign critics and reformers applaud and want to institutionalize. But as we see next, campaigns that unfold without the discipline of crisis pressure look very different indeed.

NOTES

1. Larry Bartels, "Campaign Quality: Standards for Evaluation, Benchmarks for Reform" (paper presented at the annual meeting of the American Political Science Association, Washington, D.C., 1997), pp. 26–27.
2. Jonathan Aitken, *Nixon: A Life* (Washington, D.C.: Regnery Publishing, Inc., 1993), p. 274.
3. James N. Giglio, *The Presidency of John F. Kennedy* (Lawrence, KS: University of Kansas Press, 1991), p. 17.
4. Richard M. Nixon, *Six Crises* (New York: Pyramid Books, 1962), p. 372.
5. Theodore C. Sorensen, *Kennedy* (New York: Harper & Row, 1965), p. 197.
6. Jonathan Aitken, *Nixon: A Life* (Washington, D.C.: Regnery Publishing, Inc., 1993), p. 271.
7. Gil Troy, *See How They Ran: The Changing Role of the Presidential Candidate* (New York: Free Press, 1991), p. 210.
8. Theodore C. Sorensen, *Kennedy* (New York: Harper & Row, 1965), p. 209.
9. Paul Johnson, *A History of the American People* (New York: HarperCollins, 1997), p. 854.
10. Irving Bernstein, *Promises Kept: John F. Kennedy's New Frontier* (New York: Oxford University Press, 1991), p. 37; Ithiel de Sola Pool, Robert P. Abelson, and Samuel L. Popkin, *Candidates, Issues, and Strategies: A Computer Simulation of the 1960 and 1964 Presidential Elections* (Cambridge, MA: The M.I.T. Press, 1964), p. 67.
11. Theodore C. Sorensen, *Kennedy* (New York: Harper & Row, 1965), p. 181.
12. James T. Patterson, *Grand Expectations: The United States, 1945–1974* (New York: Oxford University Press, 1996), pp. 418–422.
13. James N. Giglio, *The Presidency of John F. Kennedy* (Lawrence, KS: University of Kansas Press, 1991), p. 16.
14. Richard M. Nixon, *Six Crises* (New York: Pyramid Books, 1962), p. 365.
15. Ibid., p. 400.
16. James N. Giglio, *The Presidency of John F. Kennedy* (Lawrence, KS: University of Kansas Press, 1991), p. 17.
17. George H. Gallup, *Public Opinion 1935–1971*, vol. 3 (New York: Random House, 1972), p. 1671.
18. Ithiel de Sola Pool, Robert P. Abelson, and Samuel L. Popkin, *Candidates, Issues, and Strategies: A Computer Simulation of the 1960 and 1964 Presidential Elections* (Cambridge, MA: The M.I.T. Press, 1964), p. 86.
19. George H. Gallup, *Public Opinion 1935–1971*, vol. 3 (New York: Random House, 1972), p. 1700.
20. Richard Reeves, *President Kennedy: Profile of Power* (New York: Simon & Schuster, 1993), p. 17.
21. Herbert Stein, *Presidential Economics: The Making of Economic Policy from Roosevelt to Clinton* (Washington, D.C.: The EI Press, 1994), pp. 89–101.
22. Ibid., p. 102.
23. Irving Bernstein, *Promises Kept: John F. Kennedy's New Frontier* (New York: Oxford University Press, 1991), pp. 25, 34.
24. Theodore H. White, *The Making of the President: 1960* (New York: Atheneum, 1988), p. 389.
25. Irving Bernstein, *Promises Kept: John F. Kennedy's New Frontier* (New York: Oxford University Press, 1991).
26. Richard M. Nixon, *Six Crises* (New York: Pyramid Books, 1962), p. 333.
27. Ibid., p. 399.
28. Theodore H. White, *The Making of the President: 1960* (New York: Atheneum, 1988), p. 304.
29. Herbert Stein, *Presidential Economics: The Making of Economic Policy from Roosevelt to Clinton* (Washington, D.C.: The EI Press, 1994), pp. 93, 98–99.

30. Theodore C. Sorensen, *Kennedy* (New York: Harper & Row, 1965), pp. 470–471.
31. James N. Giglio, *The Presidency of John F. Kennedy* (Lawrence, KS: University of Kansas Press, 1991), p. 16.
32. Kathleen Hall Jamieson, *Dirty Politics: Deception, Distraction, and Democracy* (New York: Oxford, 1992), pp. 241–242.
33. Theodore C. Sorensen, *Kennedy* (New York: Harper & Row, 1965), p. 610; Arthur M. Schlesinger, *A Thousand Days: John F. Kennedy in the White House* (Boston, MA: Houghton Mifflin, 1965), p. 317.
34. Benjamin I. Page, *Choices and Echos in Presidential Elections* (Chicago, IL: University of Chicago Press, 1978), p. 156.
35. Kathleen Hall Jamieson, *Dirty Politics: Deception, Distraction, and Democracy* (New York: Oxford, 1992), pp. 243–244.
36. James T. Patterson, *Grand Expectations: The United States, 1945–1974* (New York: Oxford University Press, 1996), pp. 440–441, 466.
37. Christina Duff, "Americans' Bad Mood Finally Turns Upbeat Years after Economy," *Wall Street Journal*, 16 October 1996, p. A-1.
38. James Ceaser and Andrew Busch, *Upside Down and Inside Out: The 1992 Elections and American Politics* (Lanham, MD: Rowman and Littlefield, 1993), p. 35.
39. George Bush, letter to Bill Horner, Department of Government, University of Texas at Austin, October 1, 1998.
40. Adam Clymer, "Poll Takers Say It Was the Economy, Stupid," *New York Times*, 24 May 1993, p. A-12.
41. Alan Murray, "Economy in the U.S. Isn't Nearly as Sour as the Country's Mood," *Wall Street Journal*, 4 November 1991, p. A-1.
42. Michael Wines, "Bush Has No Plans for Major Efforts to Revive Economy," *New York Times*, 19 November 1991, p. A-1.
43. Alan Murray and John Harwood, "Bush, Sensing Only a Public Relations Problem, Will Delay Any New Economic Plans until 1992," *Wall Street Journal*, 19 November 1991, p. A-16.
44. Peter Passell, "Rudderless in the Recession," *New York Times*, 25 June 1992, p. C-2.
45. Fred Barnes, "Feeding the Beast at the White House," *Wall Street Journal*, 23 October 1995, p. A-18.
46. Jack W. Germond and Jules Witcover, *Mad as Hell: Revolt at the Ballot Box, 1992* (New York: Warner Books, 1993).
47. James Ceaser and Andrew Busch, *Upside Down and Inside Out: The 1992 Elections and American Politics* (Lanham, MD: Rowman and Littlefield, 1993).
48. David Rogers, "Armey, GOP Tough Guy in Budget Talks, Proves Good Fighter, Key Liaison to the Rank-and-File," *Wall Street Journal*, 9 January 1996, p. A-16.
49. Jack W. Germond and Jules Witcover, *Mad as Hell: Revolt at the Ballot Box, 1992* (New York: Warner Books, 1993), p. 131.
50. Kathleen A. Frankovic, "Public Opinion in the 1992 Campaign," in *The Election of 1992*, ed. Gerald M. Pomper (Chatham, NJ: Chatham House, 1993), pp. 110–131.
51. Mandy Grunwald, presentation to election debriefing conference, Annenberg School for Communication, University of Pennsylvania, December 12, 1992.
52. Robin Toner, "In 3-Way Races the Old Rules Can Trip You," *New York Times*, 5 July 1992, s-4, p. 1; David Shribman, "In a Three-Way Presidential Race, the Old Rules of Campaigning Suddenly Have Become Obsolete," *Wall Street Journal*, 27 May 1992, p. A-16.
53. T. Price, "Voters Happier about Politics at End of Angry Year, Poll Says," *Austin-American Statesman*, 15 November 1992, p. A-7.
54. Michael Feinsilber, "Battling Booklets by Bush, Clinton," *Austin American-Statesman*, 13 September 1992, p. A-14.
55. Matthew Miller, "Tsongas Left Us the Gift of Candor," *Austin American-Statesman*, 24 January 1997, p. A-15.
56. Jack W. Germond and Jules Witcover, *Mad as Hell: Revolt at the Ballot Box, 1992* (New York: Warner Books, 1993), p. 156.
57. Bruce Buchanan, "A Tale of Two Campaigns," *Political Psychology* 16 (1995), pp. 297–319.
58. Alan Murray, "Budget Gaps. The Fiscal Proposals of Bush and Clinton Both Flunk Arithmetic. Program Costs and Plans to Trim Taxes, Spending Leave Huge Shortfalls. Deficit Cuts That Aren't," *Wall Street Journal*, 15 September 1992, p. A-1.

59. Center for Media and Public Affairs, "Campaign '96: The Media and the Candidates," Final Report to the Markle Foundation (Washington, D.C.: 1998); T. Price, "Voters Happier about Politics at End of Angry Year, Poll Says," *Austin American-Statesman*, 15 November 1992, p. A-7.

60. Robin Toner, "Political Metamorphoses: Voters Impose Discipline on the Candidates as Perot Finds a New Way of Campaigning," *New York Times*, 3 November 1992, p. A-1.

STATUS QUO POLITICS

THE 1988 AND 1996 CAMPAIGNS

"Like ancient civilizations," writes Gerald Seib, "political campaigns rise up, flourish and then disintegrate into the sand, their remains to be picked over by historians and anthropologists. And like those ancient civilizations, each campaign develops its own particular language that says much about the passions and the problems of the time."[1]

If the language of 1960 and 1992 was "policy," the language of 1988 and 1996 was "business as usual." On the scale I use here, these were the bad campaigns. They are distinguished from the good by the limited attention they paid to the major public policy questions before the country, as well as by their comparatively lower voter interest and turnout figures. In the good campaigns of 1960 and 1992, truly big issues surrounding the Cold War with the Soviet Union and an escalating federal budget deficit were of paramount concern, and interest and turnout reached their highest levels in decades. But in the 1988 contest between George H. W. Bush and Michael Dukakis and the 1996, confrontation between Bill Clinton and Bob Dole the campaigns were preoccupied with such lesser matters as pollution in Boston Harbor and V-chip technology, and interest and turnout both neared record lows. The question before us, then, is: Why were 1988 and 1996 such lackluster campaigns?

1988: THE YEAR OF THE HANDLERS

Major national policy problems were abundant as the 1988 presidential election approached. One effort to cull the most important from the conference proceedings and reports of liberal, conservative, and nonpartisan issue study groups yielded a "big four" consisting of the federal budget deficit, the then-lagging international economic competitiveness of the United States, the need for clearer definition and better financing for the U.S. role in world affairs, and the ills associated with chronic domestic poverty. These were the issues that experts of varying political outlooks tended at the time to identify as most pressing.

The problems were related to one another in a variety of ways but the most compelling link was economic, with the question of affordability at the center. That made the order of importance clear. Before investments could be made in upgrading economic capacity, defense preparedness, or the self-sufficiency of the poor, the deficit would have to be tamed. The deficit was also a drag on the economy. It discouraged the use of tax cuts to stimulate the economy, and inhibited economic growth by draining investment dollars away from business activity to unproductive Treasury debt instruments.

CONTEXT

It seemed reasonable to expect that these problems would attract significant attention during the presidential campaign.[2] In fact, however, after the 1988 primaries, "which stimulated a wider and deeper discussion of issues than did the subsequent general election campaign,"[3] neither these priorities and the relations among them nor economic policy were much discussed. Only one of the four consensus priorities identified earlier—the deficit—came to be regarded, by news organizations and a minority of the electorate, as a priority for the next president. The deficit would also be the only one of the priorities to make the list of postelection policy action (see Table 5.5, page 92). But it made the list not as a campaign-generated policy signal, but in spite of having been ignored by both major party candidates during the campaign. The deficit attracted legislative action in the form of the budget agreement of 1990[4] when then-President Bush unexpectedly decided to initiate serious discussions with the Democratic Congress and to abandon his 1988 "no new taxes" pledge in order to get a serious deficit-reduction agreement. Bush deserved and got credit for initiating the agreement. But it is noteworthy that such important public business was in this instance so completely reliant on the unpredictable impulse of a president who chose not to address the problem as a candidate.

The 1988 candidates did not completely ignore the issues. As Table 5.3 (page 88) in Chapter 5 shows, several positions were taken and a few, such as George Bush's support of capital punishment and Michael Dukakis's endorsement of universal health care, became very widely known to the public. Bush operatives, sensitive to the criticism that their campaign had evaded the real issues, would claim that their candidate had advanced no fewer than 207 proposals by campaign's end.[5]

But the Bush campaign sought to focus public attention not on some lengthy list of policy proposals that they had made here and there on the campaign trail, but instead on a few carefully chosen, focus-group-tested issues and themes: capital punishment, the "Read my lips, no new taxes" pledge, and, above all, the putative failings of his opponent, governor Michael Dukakis of Massachusetts. These, not the laundry-list of issue positions, were the things that they emphasized.

BUSH ATTACKS

Dukakis was portrayed in advertising and on the stump as an idealistic liberal who was dangerously naive about crime and criminals, and out of touch with mainstream American values. With this strategy, the Bush organization would manage to sidestep much Republican vulnerability and convert the election into a "referendum on the failed policy of the governor of Massachusetts . . . rather than on the performance of the incumbent (Reagan) administration or the leadership or judgment of the G.O.P. nominee."[6]

MEDIA RESPONSE

For their part, the most visible and influential news organizations became intensely preoccupied with the sheer novelty of the Bush strategy. The power of attack ads had been fully exploited only at lower levels before 1988. Bush's was the first presidential campaign to make attacks the strategic centerpiece, the first at that level to employ coded racial appeals in their ads, and the first to so blatantly downplay the real business of the presidency.[7] The Bush campaign also successfully challenged the then-conventional political wisdom that voters would not countenance truth-stretching in one candidate's allegations against the other.[8]

Reporters with so much that was both new and provocative to cover ended up devoting most of their attention to the novelties and provocations and much less attention to pressing the candidates to clarify their stands on the problems atop the national agenda. Media coverage emphasized the horse race with a vengeance: Bush's attacks, photo-ops at flag factories, ads featuring black parolee Willie Horton (who had committed rape after being furloughed on Dukakis's watch from a Massachusetts prison), and opinion polls that confirmed the effectiveness of the Bush strategy. It was not until mid-October, when polls started showing public displeasure with the aggressive tenor of the campaign, that news stories even began to take note of that displeasure and the inaccuracies in the candidates' advertising.[9]

BUSH INCENTIVES

What allowed George Bush to abandon the issues debate of the primary season? To ignore the Reagan policy record? To give short shrift to the next president's probable leadership agenda? To downplay his own leaderly qualifications and policy vision? To, in effect, sidestep both the failings of the past and the promise of the future in order to convert the campaign and election into a referendum on the putative failings of Michael Dukakis?

The answer is a striking lack of constraints. There were, in the words of his pollster Robert Teeter, "no big peace-and-prosperity issues out there," only a wide unease about the unraveling social fabric of the country[10] that

Bush attacks on liberal permissiveness effectively exploited. The 1988 candidates faced no strong policy pressure from the electorate—which sometimes makes demands that cannot safely be ignored—to address themselves to any particular issue. The public's policy priorities for 1988 show that no single issue came to be regarded by Election Day as "most important" by as much as one-fourth of the electorate (Chapter 5, Table 5.2, page 84).

Further, the economic indicators were generally positive. That induced a measure of indifference to the presidential race. Median family income had risen 10 percent since 1981. Seventeen million new jobs had been created under Reagan. Inflation and interest rates were down. Majorities were telling pollsters that the country was on "the right track" economically.[11] The most troubling economic indicator was the out-of-control federal budget deficit, identified by just 23 percent of the public as the top problem. It was given substantial attention by elite newspapers, which not only explained the issue but also occasionally chastised the candidates for ducking it. The *Wall Street Journal*, for example, featured an issue series on what it termed the "absent agenda" highlighting the deficit and other neglected issues.[12]

VOTER DETACHMENT

But since ordinary citizens heard little of the deficit from TV news, even less from the candidates, and had no direct experience of deficit-spawned pain in their daily lives to raise the issue's profile, the limited initial public call for government attention to the problem neither expanded nor intensified. Media attention alone would help to elevate the deficit to the top rank among public priorities by campaign's end. But even though no other issue was supported by a higher percentage, the endorsement of just 23 percent was never a strong enough public signal to compel candidate attention. The candidates, knowing that a deficit-fix would require unpopular spending cuts or tax increases or both, implicitly agreed not to press the issue. "Mum's the Word on the Deficit" ran one headline.[13] In the end, public demand was never strong enough to force either candidate to discuss the deficit, or to force Bush to abandon his assault on his opponent.

FECKLESS OPPONENT

Neither was the counterpunching of the hapless Dukakis. His campaign, which has been described at length by others,[14] was unwilling to respond in kind to Bush's attacks until late in the campaign, and unable to change the subject by focusing on issues:

> Dukakis, who made a more diligent attempt to campaign on substantive issues, resisted pressure from campaign aides to go on the attack sooner

and more often, and to defend himself against Bush's assaults on his patriotism. . . . "It might be argued I should have fired back immediately" [said Dukakis] "but there would have been even less voter participation"—suggesting voters would have been even more turned off by the bickering.[15]

In sum, the situation offered nothing—no law, no compelling public demand, no effective political opposition, no ethical constraints, and no internal, moral inhibition—to stop Bush from seizing the initiative and framing the election to suit himself.

RATIONALE

Why did Bush, a man described by some political opponents as a "wimp," and known by his closest friends to prefer not just a "kinder, gentler" but also a nobler approach to public life in general, decide to unleash a carefully orchestrated, often misleading, and roundly mean-spirited attack on Michael Dukakis; an attack that would blur the policy discussion into irrelevance and frustrate and disgust much of the public?

> In part because his handlers convinced him that the other side had started it: Bush's game was horseshoes, not alley fighting; it was easier to get him down-and-dirty if you persuaded him that he had been wronged and that the manly thing to do was fight back. When he came home from his convention-week camping trip, Ailes, Atwater, and Barbara Bush were waiting with the news that the Democrats had just spent four nights punching his lights out on prime-time TV, chorusing "Where Was George?" and hooting that he had been born with a silver foot in his mouth.[16]

But the major reason that Bush swallowed his scruples was the fact that his campaign staff research showed that "going negative" was the only way to win.

Bush's own poll-proven "negatives" were high, and no positive issue or favorable Bush characteristic had enough impact when tested in focus groups or polls to counteract Bush's drawbacks, which included an indistinct image and a sixteen-point disadvantage to Dukakis in a Gallup poll taken May 13–18.

Since Ronald Reagan could not be reelected president, the next election was necessarily about a change at the top. The aim in a no-incumbent race without a voter-driven policy debate was simple: to make Bush look preferable to Dukakis as the next president. The way to do that was suggested by the famous May 1988 Paramus, New Jersey, focus groups, which gathered some thirty blue-collar and white-collar Democrats—all former Reagan supporters—to discuss the campaign.

All thirty initially planned to vote for Dukakis. But after they were told of the Massachusetts governor's veto of a 1977 Pledge of Allegiance bill and the prison furlough program that released Willie Horton, half became strongly opposed to Dukakis. Bush campaign manager Lee Atwater described his own reaction as one of those "ah-hah!" moments. "I realized right there that we had the wherewithal to win . . . and that the sky was the limit on Dukakis's negatives."[17]

QUALITY CONSEQUENCES

The results of the Bush strategy were unarguable. For Bush, there was a victory that had looked improbable six months earlier. For the handlers, there was vindication: ". . . Bush's campaign was a technical masterpiece—an example of brilliant exploitation of the new political technology."[18] But for campaign quality, the results were devastating. Most nonconsultants were appalled by the Bush strategy. The campaign left voters disgusted and indifferent to policy. Neither attracted nor inspired by the political spectacle or by personal worries connected to politics, they had little incentive to invest significant time or energy. Voter learning was therefore unimpressive (just four of twenty issue positions were correctly attributed to candidates by a majority of voters in one poll). And voter turnout—50.1 percent—was the lowest since Calvin Coolidge beat John W. Davis more than six decades earlier. As already noted, the campaign discussion would figure little in the postelection policy action (Table 5.5, page 92).

1988 IN PERSPECTIVE

"What," asked CBS anchorman Dan Rather of correspondent Ed Bradley, who was fresh from interviewing voters leaving the polls, "was [the voters'] reaction to the tone of the campaign—do they agree with the press and a lot of the pundits that it was particularly nasty?"

> "No question, Dan," said the candid Bradley . . . "a lot of people expressed the opinion . . . that this has been a very negative campaign, and that was . . . borne out by the numbers we're seeing from our exit-poll survey. Most people thought that both of the candidates spent more time attacking the other man than they did explaining their own position . . . but they blame George Bush more for that negative tone."[19]

1996: THE YEAR OF THE YAWN

Where the 1988 campaign evoked public distaste, 1996 would spawn indifference. These were, to be sure, very different reactions. But because the end results—mass "tune out" and nonparticipation, plus inattention to pressing national problems—were the same, there would be similar, largely adverse, consequences for campaign quality.

The year 1996 "will almost certainly be remembered as one of the dullest presidential campaigns in recent times . . . the boring election," wrote Adam Nagourney.[20] The signs were plentiful. Voter turnout, up sharply in 1992, fell in 1996 to scarcely 49 percent, its lowest level in 72 years. Candidate debates, usually the campaign spectacle that voters find most interesting, drew far smaller audiences than they had in 1992. The first presidential candidate debate drew a 31.6 rating, 30.6 million homes, compared to 38.3 and 35.7 million homes for the first debate in 1992. The second debate had a 21.6 rating, reaching 25.3 million homes, compared with a 1992 second-debate 46.3 rating, reaching 43.1 million homes.[21] And in a *New York Times* poll taken just over two weeks before the election, only 44 percent described the campaign as "interesting," while 50 percent called it "dull."[22] The Markle surveys show that 66 percent claimed to have made up their mind by mid-September 1996, compared with 58 percent in 1992 and just 49 percent in 1988.

Why was the campaign so widely perceived as boring? It could not have been because there was nothing of national importance for the candidates to address. As in 1988, many unresolved problems clamored for attention and might usefully have been discussed and debated at length in the campaign. The consensus among journalists, academics, and candid politicians, for example, was that it was none too early to begin debating the options for addressing the Social Security and Medicare funding shortfall sure to follow the retirement of the Baby Boomer generation beginning in 2012.[23] Other important national problems ripe for attention included campaign finance and other political system reforms, the continuing access and affordability crises of a health care system that still excluded some forty million Americans who lacked health insurance, the need for clearer definition and public validation of the U.S. role in the post–Cold War world, the fact that the United States featured the largest gap between the rich and the poor among the industrialized nations, and the question of whether and how to meet the needs of the many children thrown into poverty by the recently enacted and clearly underfunded welfare reform legislation. In short, 1996 had the potential to be more productive of needed debate, more policy-relevant and potentially much more interesting to voters, a majority of whom had personal stakes in one or more of these big questions, than it ended up being.

At least in part, the campaign was perceived as boring because the candidates simply chose not to address such controversial issues. Had they done so, they might well have attracted considerably more voter attention and interest than they did, and perhaps even generated a consensus behind a solution to one or more big problems. But that also would have introduced considerable electoral risk for both major party nominees. In the end, they did not raise such issues because, in pointed contrast to 1992, nobody—neither voters nor third-party candidates—made them do it. That left them free to ignore inconvenient problems. Lack of voter demand meant they could pick the strategies, issues, and themes they thought most likely to enhance their political fortunes. And, as former Bush budget director Richard Darman observed, that is exactly what they did: "Without providing credible proposals for spending reduction, both candidates offer the voters attractive tax cuts—what Ross Perot has termed "free candy just before elections."[24]

CONTEXT

In 1996, voters were simply not energized. No problem seemed threatening enough to drive them to political leaders in search of answers. They did not insist *en masse* that candidates address social security reform, health care, or anything else. As Table 5.2 on page 84 shows, no policy problem was embraced as a high priority by as much as 20 percent of likely voters. Three factors in particular seem to have dulled the public's sense of political urgency and insured that voters would not hold candidates' feet to the fire on issues as they had in 1992.

The first was the general strength of the economy, which by 1996 had improved visibly enough to greatly reduce the mass anxiety of 1992 and to make the 1996 presidential contest seem far less important to many whose feelings of personal vulnerability had led them to focus intently on the economy four years earlier. The second was the fact that a major political debate had arisen and been resolved just before the public campaign for president began in earnest. That debate was over budget priorities, and it did rivet the attention of the nation in 1995 and early 1996. It did so because the combatants—President Clinton and the Republican Congress—stalemated and jointly provoked two relatively brief government shutdowns. But once it was clear that the public would take the president's side in the budget fight, and accept the president's characterization of the Republicans as threats to mainstream values and associated federal programs, it would make the outcome of the upcoming campaign and election seem foreordained, and thus, anticlimactic.

The third factor was a novel and unprecedentedly early use of television advertising by the Clinton campaign, which not only helped sway the public reaction to the government shutdowns, but also helped to link the Republican nominee, former Senate majority leader Bob Dole, to the unpopular House speaker Newt Gingrich, and to the least popular portions of the Republican agenda: spending cuts in Medicare, education, and environmental protection, aimed at financing tax cuts for "the rich."

The Strong Economy Backdrop   The economy and the budget fight were related in ways that helped to settle the outcome of the election before the campaign began. The foundation of good economic news was laid by the Clinton administration's 1993 deficit reduction package, itself the culmination of the 1992 election's deficit reduction policy signal. By winning early credibility with the financial markets and the Federal Reserve interest setters, the 1993 package helped to set in motion forces that would eventually increase economic growth and restore public confidence in the economy.[25]

The public did not begin giving Clinton credit for the strong economy soon enough to prevent Republicans from capturing the Congress in 1994. Republicans were able to capitalize on the failure of the Clinton health care plan, public unhappiness with mostly Democratic Congressional incumbents, and eventual House Speaker Newt Gingrich's effective "Contract with America" strategy for nationalizing usually parochial midterm elections, to seize control.

But the 1993 budget package, which passed without a single Republican vote, did help to create the favorable economic backdrop—business confidence, low interest rates and reasonable economic growth—that would eventually frame public reaction to the great budget debates of 1995 and early 1996. Journalist Gerald Seib[26] credits Clinton Treasury Secretary Robert Rubin, who pressed Clinton to abandon his 1992 middle-class tax cut pledge in the face of greater-than-expected deficit figures before he was even inaugurated. "You mean to tell me that the success of the program and my reelection hinges on the Federal Reserve and a bunch of . . . bond traders?" Mr. Clinton complained, according to a later book by Bob Woodward. The answer was yes, and the result was a deficit cutting package that calmed the markets, reassured the Fed, and helped make it possible for Clinton to benefit from a 63 percent reduction in the deficit during his first term.

The Budget Fight   The real fight for the presidency thus began with the Republican victory in 1994 and ended in late 1995 and early 1996, when Clinton vetoed the Republican budgets, the Republicans shut down the government, and people began making it clear to pollsters that they rejected much of the Republican agenda and favored Clinton as a check against Republican "extremism."

As part of his strategy for political survival that would come to be known as "triangulation," Clinton embraced the popular parts of the Republican agenda, including a balanced budget within seven years and a stringent version of welfare reform that alienated the liberal wing of the Democratic party. But he took a strong stand against those Republican priorities—cuts in Medicare, Medicaid, education, and environmental protection—that he knew to be unpopular, enabling him to marginalize the Republicans and capture the political middle ground. Opined the *New York Times*: "Campaign historians will probably identify the day the Government shut down as the day Mr. Clinton began his political revival."[27] But it was not until later that Mr. Clinton, with an artful collection of speeches and radio addresses, began to climb in the polls.[28] He did so because he was able to capitalize on the shutdowns, using them convincingly as evidence that the Republicans were "radicals" willing not only to shut down the government but also to cut Medicare spending to finance tax cuts for the wealthy.

The Preseason Ad Campaign   The third reason why the 1996 campaign seemed in retrospect to have been "over before it started" had to do with Clinton's unprecedentedly early television advertising campaign. Realistically fearful that the 1994 Republican capture of Congress would invite Democratic primary challengers, Clinton pressed the Democratic National Committee to initiate its largest-ever "soft money" fund-raising program. Use of DNC soft money enabled Clinton to finance a hugely expensive early-start ad campaign, seemingly without violating the legal campaign spending limits for candidates. It also permitted him to keep his personal campaign treasury large enough to fend off several potential challengers for the Democratic nomination who had been inspired by Clinton's many pre-1995 political weaknesses.

Thus protected from challengers, and well before the budget shutdown confrontations with Congress began, Clinton initiated, in July of 1995, a sixteen-month ad campaign in twenty key swing states. Revulsion against the "Willie Horton" negativism of 1988 was still fueling antipolitical sentiment in 1996. This led Clinton to devise a strategy of deploying attack advertising not only unprecedentedly early, but outside the major media markets, thereby staying "under the radar" of media critics poised to denounce negative politics.[29] Thus, the campaign avoided such ad markets as New York, Washington, D.C., and, to a lesser extent, Los Angeles, the three cities where most nationally oriented journalists live and work. With few exceptions, the news media did not focus on candidate advertising until late in the campaign, a fact in part attributable to the general reduction in the amount of media coverage in comparison with 1992 and 1988.[30]

The keys to the success of the Clinton ads, according to his political strategist Dick Morris, were to advertise on current legislative issues only (thus ensuring their immediate relevance to voters despite the multimonth distance from the election), to advertise only the positions that focus groups showed the public agreed with already, and, in order to avoid legal-spending-limit caps, to avoid explicitly promoting Clinton's candidacy. The latter move was intended to legitimize DNC financing, permitting it to spend some $85 million in unregulated soft money, more than twice as much as any single candidate had spent on advertising in 1992.

The first ads dealt with Clinton's resistance to the Republican wish to repeal the ban on assault rifles. The second ad wave, deployed in August of 1995, criticized Republican budget cuts and promoted the president's balanced-budget plan. For the remaining months before the election, ads were tailored to address the proposed Republican reductions that Clinton research showed mattered most to voters: Medicare, Medicaid, education, and environmental protection:

One typical commercial running in April 1996, in Lansing, Michigan, said
Mr. Clinton wanted to "preserve Medicare" and "save anti-drug programs."
But Speaker Newt Gingrich and Bob Dole, the Senate Majority leader and
then the leading Republican candidate for President, were out to block him,
the narrator warned, "Dole-Gingrich vote no—no to America's families."[31]

Clinton managed, in designing the ads, to reconfigure attack advertising so as
to reap its benefits while avoiding its costs.[32] His ads savaged Dole for months
while praising Clinton. Clinton personally never uttered an unkind word.[33]
The success of the ad campaign was apparent in various polling results made
available near the end of the campaign. For example, an October 17–20 *New
York Times* poll showed 73 percent viewed Clinton as above the fray, spending more time explaining his plans than attacking Bob Dole.[34] With Election
Day looming, Clinton was finally getting credit from voters for the good economy, and for the feeling that the country was headed in the right direction.[35]
And a mid-October *New York Times* poll showed the public remained deeply
suspicious of Republican plans on Medicare, with 56 percent saying they dis-
approved and only 25 percent approving.[36] Women voters in particular rejected the Republican position, and they also reject the Republican social
agenda, as symbolized by the abortion issue.

Inexplicably, the Republicans never answered the early ads, even though
Clinton internal polling showed significant differences between voters' attitudes in the advertised states and the solid Democratic or Republican states
where no ads were televised. Had Republicans responded in kind, the Clinton advantage might have been neutralized, since Republicans had the capacity to outspend Democrats. But by March, Mr. Dole had exhausted his
primary-season funding fighting off GOP challengers. A lot of the negative
charges that were thrown at Dole came from fellow Republicans during the
primary season. A Steve Forbes ad, for example, said: "Bob Dole, deceiving
voters. A Washington politician. It's time for a change."[37] When Dole did begin
to return Clinton's fire relatively late in the campaign, it made him look like
the negative one to the public, and voters began to complain.[38] The Clinton
campaign, recognizing an opportunity, regularly accused Dole of being the
aggressor, a tactic that "drove the Dole campaign crazy."[39] The Clinton tactic
worked. An October *New York Times* poll showed that 63 percent saw him as
spending more time attacking Clinton than explaining his own policies.[40]

Morris further reports that internal polling showed that voters eventually preferred the president's budget plan to the Republican version by more
than two to one, and "trusted Clinton to balance the budget in a way that is
fair to all over the Republicans by twelve to fifteen points."[41] Morris concludes
that the early advertising was one of four keys to Clinton's victory, and reports claiming to insiders that the election was over a full year before Election
Day, in large part because of the advertising. The other three Morris keys involved Clinton moves to neutralize Republican wedge issues—e.g., Clinton's
acceptance of the balanced-budget goal in June 1995; the State of the Union

speech in 1996 declaring that "the era of big government is over," and his signing of the welfare reform bill the same year.[42] Corroboration of Morris's claim that the election was over before it started was later added by Bob Dole himself, who, in written testimony to a Senate committee in 1998, said that, "History will show that, because of the ad campaign, the election—for all practical purposes—was decided by early 1996, long before Republicans had a nominee.[43]

CAMPAIGN DYNAMICS

By the time Bob Dole had amassed enough primary delegates to lock up the Republican nomination in late March he was well aware that his prospects were grim. From then until Election Day, Clinton's high approval ratings would hold, giving him what would prove to be an overwhelming advantage. But competitive or not, the general election campaign still had to be fought. And the expectation of a rout had important consequences for the kind of campaign it would be. One such consequence was a sharp decline in attention to the race. Another was that candidates would avoid the real national agenda to search instead for "candy for voters before elections," that is, any lure strong enough to amass a winning vote share in what was sure to be a low-turnout election.

The Attention Deficit In 1992, Texas billionaire Ross Perot made himself into the major attraction of the presidential campaign, drawing attention to the campaign and building interest in the economic policy debate. Not only did he increase the already high salience of the budget deficit to voters, and thus single-handedly increase the likelihood of a postelection deficit-reduction effort, he also contributed to the upsurge in voter turnout.[44] But despite the tantalizing possibility of another historic outsider candidacy, in the end there would be no comparably high-profile attractions at work to help stimulate either policy momentum or citizen participation. The result would be an attention deficit.

With the leading candidates avoiding the most provocative questions, the best chance for an upsurge in public attention and interest in 1996 was the potential candidacy of retired general and former Joint Chiefs of Staff Chair Colin Powell. The latest of the nonpolitical outsiders to capture America's fancy, Powell had dominated the "invisible primary" season as he toured the nation in 1995 promoting his memoirs, striking fear in the hearts of presidential hopefuls everywhere. Some analysts believed that Powell, who did not even disclose that he was a Republican until the day he announced that he would not seek elective office in 1996, might have succeeded as an Independent.[45] But his lack of interest made that possibility moot. It also denied the 1996 campaign an otherwise certain explosion of media coverage. Powell's withdrawal disappointed millions and delivered a major blow to enthusiasm for the race.[46]

The only other hope for a surge in public attention was if Ross Perot could stage a comeback. Working steadily in the aftermath of 1992, he and his supporters had managed to get his Reform party on all fifty state ballots in preparation for another run for the presidency in 1996. It soon became apparent, however, that Perot was not to be the attraction in 1996 that he had been four years earlier. His stature had been tarnished in the interim by his increasingly quirky behavior, and his attractiveness diminished by a less supportive press and public and a much less promising issue environment. His fading appeal was apparent in the reaction to his first 1996 half-hour infomercial. It aired on September 1, 1996, ranked just 104th among the week's 107 prime-time television programs, and was seen in fewer than two million households, according to Nielson Media Research. By contrast, Perot's October 6 infomercial debut in 1992 tied for 32nd place among 90 prime-time programs, and was seen in 11.2 million households.[47] Perot's standing in the 1996 polls declined from highs near 18 percent in early spring to single-digit levels near Election Day. Still, it is conceivable that he might have intensified public interest in the campaign once again, had the networks permitted him to purchase more prime advertising time[48] and had he been allowed to participate in the candidate debates. But that was prevented by the Commission on Presidential Debates, a bipartisan group headed by former chairmen of the Democratic and Republican parties. The Commission recommended against including Perot and other third-party candidates because "they [had] no realistic chance to win the election." The commission was dissuaded by polls showing Perot's support at less than 10 percent, adding that, "Participation is not extended to candidates because they might prove interesting or entertaining."[49] Perot claimed he was down in the polls because Republicans and Democrats insured his exclusion from the debates, thus preventing him from getting his message across.[50]

Reduced Media Coverage   Faced with the prospect of a lackluster policy debate and with neither Colin Powell nor Ross Perot as feature attractions, news media organizations reduced campaign coverage dramatically, and with it the chance of building a larger audience for the campaign. Markle-sponsored coding by the Center for Media and Public Affairs (CMPA) showed that the major networks substantially curtailed their election coverage. ABC, CBS and NBC offered 45 percent less election news in 1996 than in 1992. There were less dramatic declines at PBS (22 percent) and the *Wall Street Journal* (21 percent). Within CMPA's sample, only the *New York Times* increased its coverage from 1992 levels. Such coverage as there was during the fall campaign tended to emphasize the contest and the conflict between the candidates, as shown in Chapter 1, Table 1.1, page 12. For an election campaign already widely regarded as noncompetitive, that was not a coverage pattern calculated to attract public attention and increase interest.

To this was added a generally negative coverage tone. CMPA coding showed that the candidates' speeches and advertising were much more positive than portrayed in news accounts.[51]

Issue Miniaturization   Later, when it was finally over, one analyst would conclude that the 1996 presidential campaign could have been

> an exercise in high policy clarification: What the people might have ap-
> proved this year—had Mr. Dole and Mr. Clinton been more obliging—was
> either of the competing views of government presented by House Repub-
> licans in 1994 or by the more governmentally ambitious Mr. Clinton who
> ran in 1992.[52]

In fact, this was never a real possibility, for as we have seen; neither major party nominee had any reason whatever to encourage the voters to think of their choices in such fundamental terms. As the leading candidates saw it, all the incentives pointed *away* from big, controversial policy questions. Instead, their featured proposals would be carefully chosen to appeal to the personal interests rather than the broader public concerns of specific groups of what they deemed to be reachable voters. Clinton, needing only to protect an al- ready comfortable lead over Dole, avoided much discussion of the hard pres- idential choices to come. Except for occasionally reminding voters of past achievements like deficit reduction and welfare reform, his emphasis would be on focus-group-tested *small initiatives* aimed at the concerns that dominat- ed the private lives of target voters. Table 5.3 (page 88) and Table 5.4 (page 90) in Chapter 5 list many of the best known examples, and demonstrate the suc- cess of the ploy. For example, the three most widely supported candidate issue positions in the week before the election were Clinton positions: a proposal to spend $2.75 billion to improve the reading skills of school children in grades K–3, endorsed by 71 percent of respondents; a proposed $3.4 billion package of tax breaks and other incentives to encourage businesses to create jobs for people leaving the welfare rolls, endorsed by 67 percent; and a "targeted tax cut" proposal aimed at poor working families and middle-class families with children, as well as tax credits for college tuition, all to be financed with spe- cific budget cuts. This proposal was supported by 66 percent of respondents to a Markle Foundation–Princeton Survey Research Associates poll taken in the days just before the election.

Dole's call for a 15 percent across-the-board tax cut had the distinction of being recognized as his by the largest group of respondents, 59 percent. And it was endorsed in the Markle survey by some 51 percent (Table 5.4, page 90). But in an October *Wall Street Journal* poll,[53] respondents opposed it 46 to 34 per- cent, down from an August survey showing the proposal to have been en- dorsed by a plurality, 39 to 32. Why didn't this proposal, chosen as the centerpiece of the Dole campaign on the theory that people will vote to keep more of their own money, work better for him? Opponents interviewed in the *Wall Street Journal* survey said it was simply too blatant a pander, given Dole's long record of opposition to just such tax cuts, and bad policy to boot, given the still-sizable federal budget deficits in place at the time. Too, Clinton had long since successfully portrayed Republican tax cuts as hurtful to Medicare, Medicaid, education, and the environment. Finally, voters didn't believe they would actually get a tax cut, because the last two politicians to promise tax relief—Bush and Clinton—had been unable to deliver. In the end, neither this nor anything else that Dole tried served to shake loose enough independent voters to give Dole a fighting chance.[54]

CONCLUSION

Campaigns are shaped by their circumstances. The interplay among candidates, journalists, and voters is inevitably affected by the presence or absence of such pressing problems as recessions and threats to national security. That is why the four cases, whose main features are summed in Tables 3.1 and 3.2, display the variation that they do. The 1960 and 1992 campaigns unfolded while public anxiety over threats to peace and prosperity was high, and the candidates had little choice but to respond. The years 1988 and 1996, on the other hand, show what happens when mass anxieties do *not* arise to energize

TABLE 3.1   CONTEXT-INCENTIVE INTERACTIONS:
1960 AND 1992 PRESIDENTIAL CAMPAIGNS

CONTEXT	INCENTIVES
1960	
Tense Soviet relationship	Voters: demand better Soviet relations
Consensus on top priority	Candidates: stress peace through strength; note economic/civil rights plans
Civil rights stirrings	Media: cover policy choices
Mild economic slowdown	
1992	
"Bad" economic indicators	Voters: demand economic reassurance
Consensus on top priority	Candidates: stress detailed economic solutions; avoid/disguise attacks
Dissatisfaction with incumbent	Media: cover Perot and his signature issues
Antipolitical mood	
Three major candidates	

TABLE 3.2   CONTEXT-INCENTIVE INTERACTIONS:
1988 AND 1996 PRESIDENTIAL CAMPAIGNS

CONTEXT	INCENTIVES
1988	
Good economic indicators	Voters: detach/avoid
No consensus policy pressure	Candidates: issue opportunism; attack, discredit opponent
	Media: cover Bush attacks
1996	
Very good economic indicators	Voters: detach/disinterest
No consensus policy pressure	Candidates: issue opportunism; disguised attacks
Antipolitical mood	Media: reduced coverage

campaigns and tie the hands of the candidates. There is reversion to a norm in which candidates may safely pursue self-serving agendas that do not clarify national priorities and do not inspire high rates of voter engagement.

What can be said of these differences? We can say that they are predictable expressions of human nature. Rational candidates will do only what is necessary to get elected, and rational citizens will absorb the costs of acquiring information and voting only when the perceived benefits justify the effort. Attempts to override these tendencies with reforms have had disappointing results. The many expansions of the right to vote, for example, such as the 26th Amendment extending that right to those eighteen years of age, have not had the hoped-for impact on turnout. Neither has the 1993 National Voter Registration Act, the so-called "Motor Voter" law, which made voter registration significantly easier throughout the nation. And innovations like free network television time for presidential candidates—offered in the hope of inspiring more substantive discussion of important national issues—have done little to change candidate behavior. It is noteworthy that both the Motor Voter law and the free TV time experiments had their first major opportunity to alter candidate and voter behavior in 1996. Worthy though they were, these initiatives did not displace the incentives that yielded a big drop in turnout and the candidate issue evasion described earlier. Reversion to *status quo* politics in ordinary times, if not inevitable, remains a stubbornly high probability.

There may be, as I argue in the final chapter, more promising ways to rebalance the political incentive system to encourage good campaigns in ordinary times. But even those who believe that a high incidence of bad campaigns is inevitable can take solace from the key teaching of the previous chapter's good campaign cases: that crisis improves the quality of campaigns when it really matters. This is a persuasive conclusion. But the implicit corollary—namely that quality can safely be ignored in noncrisis circumstances because then it *doesn't* really matter—is far less persuasive. It is plausible enough, however, to require explicit rebuttal. For if it is true, then why should anyone worry at all about the policy focus of the average campaign or the voter turnout for a run-of-the-mill election? Why is it, exactly, that campaign quality *cannot* prudently be ignored outside crisis circumstances? These questions concern us next.

NOTES

1. Gerald F. Seib, "Political Words: Tales of Bosses, Extremists, Newt," *Wall Street Journal*, 3 July 1996, p. A-12.
2. Bruce Buchanan, "The New Presidential Leadership Agenda" (paper presented at the annual meeting of the American Political Science Association, Washington, D.C., 1988).
3. Alexander Heard, *Made in America: Improving the Nomination and Election of Presidents* (New York: HarperCollins, 1991), p. 29.
4. Howard E. Shuman, *Politics and the Budget*, 3rd ed. (Englewood Cliffs, NJ: Prentice-Hall, 1992), p. 304.
5. Peter Goldman and Tom Mathews, *The Quest for the Presidency: The 1988 Campaign* (New York: Simon & Schuster, 1989), p. 355.
6. Norman J. Ornstein and Mark Schmitt, "The 1988 Election," *Foreign Affairs* 68 (1989), p. 44.
7. Peter Goldman and Tom Mathews, *The Quest for the Presidency: The 1988 Campaign* (New York: Simon & Schuster, 1989), p. 360.
8. Kathleen Hall Jamieson, "Is Truth Now Irrelevant in Presidential Campaigns?" *Washington Post National Weekly Edition*, 7–13 November 1988, p. 28.
9. Bruce Buchanan, *Electing a President: The Markle Commission Research on Campaign '88* (Austin, TX: University of Texas Press, 1991), p. 69.
10. Peter Goldman and Tom Mathews, *The Quest for the Presidency: The 1988 Campaign* (New York: Simon & Schuster, 1989), p. 362.
11. Elizabeth Drew, *Election Journal: Political Events of 1987–1988* (New York: William Morrow, 1989), pp. 272–273.
12. Bruce Buchanan, *Electing a President: The Markle Commission Research on Campaign '88* (Austin, TX: University of Texas Press, 1991), p. 59.
13. Paul Taylor, "The Bush-Dukakis Pact: Mum's the Word on the Deficit," *Washington Post National Weekly Edition*, 30 May–5 June, 1988.
14. Jack W. Germond and Jules Witcover, *Whose Broad Stripes and Bright Stars? The Trivial Pursuit of the Presidency 1988* (New York: Warner Books, 1989); Peter Goldman and Tom Mathews, *The Quest for the Presidency: The 1988 Campaign* (New York: Simon & Schuster, 1989).
15. Jack W. Germond and Jules Witcover, *Whose Broad Stripes and Bright Stars? The Trivial Pursuit of the Presidency 1988* (New York: Warner Books, 1989), p. 465.
16. Peter Goldman and Tom Mathews, *The Quest for the Presidency: The 1988 Campaign* (New York: Simon & Schuster, 1989), p. 356.
17. Quoted in Paul Taylor and David S. Broder, "How the Presidential Campaign Got Stuck on the Low Road," *Washington Post National Weekly Edition*, 7–13 November 1988, p. 14.
18. Paul Taylor, "Pigsty Politics: The 1988 Presidential Race Set a New Standard for Negative Ads," *Washington Post National Weekly Edition*, 13–19 February 1989, p. 14.
19. Richard Ben Cramer, *What It Takes* (New York: Random House, 1992), p. 1021.
20. Adam Nagourney, "The Year of the Yawn," *New York Times*, 3 November 1996, sec. 4, p. 1-A.

21. Ed Bark, "Presidential Debate Draws Record Low Ratings Nationwide," *Dallas Morning News*, 18 October 1996, p. 20-A.
22. Richard L. Berke, "Should Dole Risk Tough Image? Poll Says He Already Has One," *New York Times*, 16 October 1996, p. A-1.
23. David E. Rosenbaum, "Past Is No Guide to Stands Taken by Dole and Clinton This Year," *New York Times*, 8 September 1996, p. 21.; Richard Darman, "If We Were Serious," *New York Times*, 1 September 1996, sec. 4, p. 9.
24. Richard Darman, "If We Were Serious," *New York Times*, 1 September 1996, sec. 4, p. 9.
25. Robert E. Rubin, "The Clinton Growth Plan," *Wall Street Journal*, 31 October 1996, p. A-22.
26. Gerald F. Seib, "Clinton's Gamble: How It Shaped the '96 Race," *Wall Street Journal*, 30 October 1996, p. A-20.
27. "Campaign '96, R.I.P.," *New York Times*, 3 November 1996, sec. 4, p. 14.
28. James Ceaser and Andrew Busch, *Losing to Win: The 1996 Elections and American Politics* (Lanham, MD: Rowman and Littlefield, 1997), p. 44.
29. Keven Goldman, "TV Will Be a Winner in the '96 Elections," *Wall Street Journal*, 14 July 1995, p. B-8.
30. Center for Media and Public Affairs, "Executive Summary," Final Report to the Markle Foundation (Washington, D.C.: 1998), p. 4.
31. James Bennet, "Justice Dept. Questions President in '96 Campaign Finance Inquiry," *New York Times*, 10 November 1998, p. A-1.
32. James Bennet, "Clinton Makes Use of Negative Ads," *New York Times*, 22 October 1996, p. A-12.
33. Alison Mitchell, "Leaving Aides to Duel Dole, President Stresses Education," *New York Times*, 22 October 1996, p. A-13.
34. Richard L. Berke, "Aggressive Turn by Dole Appears to Be Backfiring," *New York Times*, 22 October 1996, p. A-1.
35. Ronald G. Shafer, "Washington Wire," *Wall Street Journal*, 25 October 1996, p. A-1.
36. Adam Clymer, "G.O.P. Pushes Congress Strategy That Shuns Dole," *New York Times*, 23 October 1996, p. A-1.
37. Susan Feeney, "Dole Team Says Image Doesn't Fit the True Man," *Dallas Morning News*, 30 October 1996, p. A-1.
38. Princeton Survey Research Associates, *The 1996 Markle Election Watch Surveys: A Report on the Findings* (Princeton, NJ: 1997).
39. James Bennet, "Clinton Makes Use of Negative Ads," *New York Times*, 22 October 1996, p. A-12.
40. Richard L. Berke, "Aggressive Turn by Dole Appears to Be Backfiring," *New York Times*, 22 October 1996, p. A-1.
41. Dick Morris, *Behind the Oval Office* (New York: Random House, 1997), p. 151.
42. Ibid., p. 149.
43. Bob Dole, "The Election Was Decided by Early 1996," *Wall Street Journal*, 15 January 1998, p. A-18.
44. Dean Lacy and Barry C. Burden, "The Vote-Stealing and Turnout Effects of Ross Perot in the 1992 Presidential Election," *American Journal of Political Science* 43 (1999), pp. 233–255; Bruce Buchanan, "A Tale of Two Campaigns," *Political Psychology* 16 (1995), pp. 297–319; Theodore J. Lowi, "The Dog That Did Not Bark: Ross Perot and the Prospects for a Permanent Third Party," *Extensions* (spring 1993), pp. 8–11; Adam Clymer, "Turnout on Election Day '92 Was the Largest in 24 Years," *New York Times*, 17 December 1992, p. A-13.
45. Jeff Greenfield, "Seizing the Middle Ground," *New York Times*, 9 October 1995, p. A-11.
46. A. M. Rosenthal, "The Powell Point," *New York Times*, 10 November 1995, p. A-17.
47. Ed Bark, "Perot Rewriting Rules on TV Campaigning," *Dallas Morning News*, 10 September 1996, p. A-6.
48. Lori Stahl, "Perot Complains to FCC about Ad Time," *Dallas Morning News*, 25 September 1996, p. A-6.
49. John Harwood, "Panel Recommends Excluding Perot from Debates," *Wall Street Journal*, 18 September 1996, p. A-6.
50. B. Drummond Ayres, "Perot Again Stokes Up His Third Party Themes," *New York Times*, 3 November 1997, p. A-16.

51. Center for Media and Public Affairs, "Executive Summary," Final Report to the Markle Foundation (Washington, D.C.: 1998), p. 5.
52. Adam Nagourney, "The Year of the Yawn," *New York Times*, 3 November 1996, sec. 4, p. A-1.
53. Ronald G. Shafer, "Washington Wire," *Wall Street Journal*, 25 October 1996, p. A-1.
54. Alison Mitchell, "Stung by Defeats in '94, Clinton Regrouped and Co-Opted G.O.P. Strategies," *New York Times*, 7 November 1996, p. B-1.

WHY QUALITY MATTERS

C risis or not, good presidential campaigns are useful. Their contributions to the health of the American polity are just as valuable in ordinary times as in difficult times. I will show later that three important benefits result from campaigns that clarify important policy priorities and choices and that stimulate high voter turnout on Election Day. The benefits are authoritative policy ratification; affirmation of democratic values, and a regime-bonding experience for voters.

Though related in various ways, these benefits are distinct enough and the contributions that they make are varied and complex enough to warrant separate attention and explanation. I offer both in this chapter.

GOOD CAMPAIGNS RATIFY POLICY

Good election campaigns support effective government by legitimizing policy, sometimes in ways that resolve system-threatening conflicts, sometimes in less portentous but still useful ways. Both are essential in good times and bad, and both are enhanced by policy-relevant, high-turnout campaigns. My first assertion—*turnout matters*—applies in one way or another to all three of the contributions made by good campaigns. The point to be made on this score here, however, is that the power of elections to legitimize policy via "the consent of the governed" is weakened by low voter turnout; especially turnout that dips below the symbolically significant majority level.

What of those who argue that low voter turnout is either healthy or inconsequential? Among them are Berelson et al.,[1] who contend that limited citizen participation and apathy contribute stability to the political system by cushioning the shock of disagreement, adjustment, and change. Dahl[2] extends Berelson and company by suggesting the possibly destabilizing consequences of increasing the participation of the lower socioeconomic orders of society. More recently, Rosenstone and Hansen[3] argue that "despite the surface appeal of the idea that Americans have turned off and tuned out of politics, there is in fact no evidence that popular participation in elections constitutes a display of public confidence (or lack of it) in the political system." My response to these views is simple: They are mistaken. The reason is that they take no account of the damage to policy legitimacy, democratic values, or civic integration that low turnout can cause. Teixeira addresses the legitimacy problem:

> [Consider the] problem of democratic legitimacy. As fewer and fewer people vote, the extent to which government truly rests on the consent of the governed is eroded. As a result, elected officials may not believe they have sufficient legitimacy to pursue desired policies, and citizens may believe that government is not legitimate enough to merit support. The result of this lack of confidence could be anything from widespread social and political disorganization to the reinforcement of some of the milder social pathologies we already see: gridlocked government and a political culture that turns talented people away from careers in public service.[4]

What do elections legitimize? The authority of those elected to assume power, of course. But also, when campaigns and elections make them apparent, the *policy actions* the next government will be expected to take.

HISTORY

The importance of this service to the success of American government first became apparent in the early days of the republic when the urgent need for a way to resolve bitter policy disputes short of warfare emerged. Examples of such disputes include Washington's controversial Neutrality Proclamation of 1793, the political storm raised by the actions of the French ambassador known as Citizen Genet, and the heated confrontation over Jay's Treaty with Great Britain. Initially, leaders like George Washington thought it would be possible to resolve such controversies by seeking a reasoned consensus among elites. The alternative was *faction*, which they saw as a dangerous threat to the orderly consensual government they greatly preferred. It soon became apparent, however, that men like Alexander Hamilton and Thomas Jefferson, both members of President Washington's cabinet, could not reach agreement on such fundamental questions of political philosophy and public policy as the proper scope of governmental authority or how to strengthen the economy. Realizing this, they sought allies among their colleagues in government. And as the conflict intensified and spread, the antagonists began turning to the people for support in what had become a contest for validation.

With contending elites unexpectedly in need of public help, the people's role in the political system suddenly took on a new dimension:

> . . . these campaigns to legitimize the respective positions had a catalytic effect in politicizing popular opinion. For as the public men organized themselves

into two conflicting, bitterly competitive, and mutually intolerant concep-
tions of the national good, and as the people were asked to participate in
public meetings and to support resolutions, they were, in effect, asked to take
a more active political role by throwing their support to one side or another.[5]

These were among the very first efforts to prepare the American voter to
engage in what has long since been standard electoral practice: taking sides
and resolving policy disputes by voting. But few have appreciated the extent
to which these early antagonists—the Federalists and the Democratic-Republicans—viewed each other as *saboteurs* of the original consensus on which
the Constitution was based.[6] During the "critical days" leading up to the election of 1800, "public men considered violence and the destruction of the union
as distinct and even likely possibilities."[7] It was not until the decades after
the presidential election of 1800, which tested whether angry Federalists
would allow Jefferson and the Democratic-Republicans to assume presidential and Congressional power peacefully (they grudgingly did), that it became
clear that strong partisan differences might be contested and resolved—by
the voters in presidential elections—short of revolution and bloodshed. To
demonstrate this conflict resolution potential was the great achievement of
the presidential election of 1800. Voters showed they could resolve policy disputes peacefully by formally approving one of the disputed options.

In these cases as in others, resolving conflicts meant choosing policy.
Presidential elections like 1800, 1828, 1860, 1896, 1932, 1980, and 2000 each
produced major changes in policy direction and often resolutions of bitter
power struggles as well. The nineteenth century launching of the Jefferson-
ian and Jacksonian eras made it clear that elections could be policy-relevant
on a grand scale, as Jefferson systematically dismantled the powerful Fed-
eralist policy regime and Jackson gutted the Bank of the United States. Lin-
coln's 1860 election prefigured the Civil War and the end of slavery. The
election of William McKinley in 1896 set the stage for higher tariffs, the gold
standard, and international expansion. The year 1932 brought Franklin D.
Roosevelt and the Social Security system, and 1980 ushered in the Reagan
era and massive tax and budget cuts. The 2000 election brought another historic tax cut and a sea-change in American foreign policy. Not all of these
changes had been clearly advertised during the campaigns that preceded
them. But evolving political party "systems" and practices did introduce and
eventually institutionalized a role for policy in presidential campaigns. As
early as 1840, for example, nominees were routinely associated with party
positions defined in platforms and local resolutions. This established the idea
that party and candidate policy intentions were to be included in the prospective calculations of voters, with a chance to influence the voting choice. In the
later years of the nineteenth century, party politics and the often demagogic
appeals that resulted came under fire. During this period, nomination acceptance letters from the candidates would eclipse party platforms as the

preferred guide to the policy intentions of the candidates. The *New York World* reported that most people did not "hold a candidate responsible" for fatuous party compromises; the candidate made his own platform in his letter of acceptance. But however candidates made their intentions clear, preelection disclosure was increasingly expected. "In 1880 the *New York Tribune* pronounced that candidates whose opinions were wholly unknown could no longer win."[8]

Out of these developments, the Progressive Era, and the emergence of modern political science would come the twentieth-century "responsible party" perspective, whose adherents

> expect presidents to enter office with policy proposals, perhaps even with a vision. By this perspective, good elections grant mandates, and mandates imply agendas . . . election results are typically read for their effects on the agenda of government. In fact, when the issue content is obscure, as in 1984 or 1988, most analysts are critical of the candidates, the political parties, and even the system and often call for reform . . . people expect, want, and demand that issue definition be the central purpose of elections. . . .[9]

RESOLVING POLICY QUESTIONS

So, policy-relevant presidential campaigns can be found throughout American history. But they are not inevitable because in the modern environment many candidates will avoid them if they can. That points up our problem here. Conflict over policy cannot be resolved by elections unless the campaigns that precede them are about the policies in dispute. Further, the authority of the policy signal that emerges is affected by the size of voter turnout. That is why good campaigns, which feature policy and participation, are so well-suited to clarifying and ratifying policy choices.

What of the claim that they can do so in both placid and troubled times? True, the previous examples from the early republic and later come mostly from times of high anxiety. But as I suggested when discussing the cases of 1988 and 1996, there are *always* pressing national problems—in normal *and* in trying times. And they stand to benefit from a serious airing before a large national audience that can be counted on to show up at the polls and help settle the question. Call it "conflict resolution" if you like, in trying times, and simply "policy choice" in less unsettled times. But whatever it is called, the service to effective government is basically the same—to help resolve questions about what should be done, as well as who should do it.

The matter of who governs will be settled regardless of the nature of the campaign preceding the election. But the choice of what to do is left entirely to the president and Congress *unless the presidential candidates have clarified the options for addressing high priority problems during the campaign.* The question, then, is not if an airing of the options for dealing with high-priority problems would generally be useful; it is hard to imagine when it would not be. The question is whether a trigger more orderly than crisis and mass anxiety can be found to goad candidates into facing and debating the hard choices.

Good Campaigns Affirm Democracy

The second reason why high-quality campaigns are perennially useful is that by their nature they signal a higher-than-usual level of respect for the rights, sensibilities, and needs of the electorate. This matters because the effect is to affirm democratic values, and that can help to counteract antipolitical sentiment. Antipolitical sentiment of various kinds is driving Americans away from politics at rates that some find alarming.[10] My reading of the evidence presented next is that many voters reject politics for the reasons set out in Chapter 1: because they feel neither respected nor rewarded enough by the process to justify the effort needed to become involved.

Political Discontent

Evidence that Americans are souring on politics has mounted substantially in recent decades.[11] The cross-time fortunes of three indicators closely related to support for the political system are especially relevant: voter turnout, trust in government, and faith in elections, charted in Figures 4.1, 4.2, and 4.3, respectively (see page 64 for Figures 4.2 and 4.3).

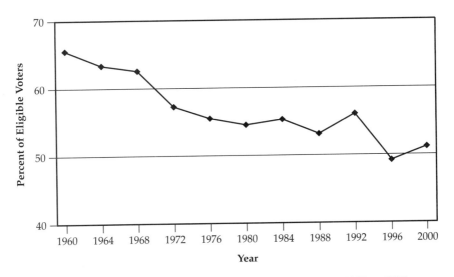

Figure 4.1 **Voter Turnout in Presidential Elections, 1960 to 2000**

Source: Figure based on data from the U.S. Federal Election Commission.

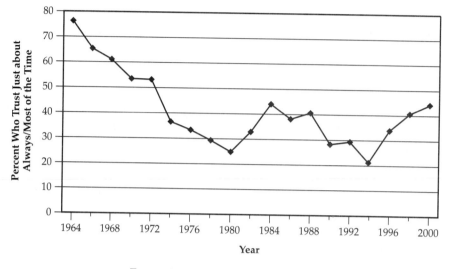

FIGURE 4.2 TRUST IN GOVERNMENT

Source: American National Election Studies (University of Michigan).

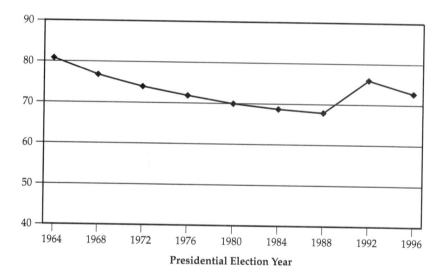

FIGURE 4.3 FAITH IN ELECTIONS

"How much do you feel that having elections makes the government pay attention to what the people think—a good deal, some, or not much?"

NES sample averages for presidential election years 1964–1996, adjusted for question order, panel status, and date of interview. Quantities displayed for each election year are average values on a 0-to-100 scale; "good deal" = 100; "some" = 50; "not much" = 0.

Source: Larry M. Bartels, "Question Order and Declining Faith in Elections," *Public Opinion Quarterly* 66 (2002), pp. 67–79. Reprinted by permission of the author.

VOTER TURNOUT

Although the precise meaning of the turnout for any particular election is open to argument, it is hard not to interpret the trend-line in voting-age population turnout in presidential elections between 1960 (62.8 percent) and 2000 (51 percent) as less-than-supportive citizen behavior (see Figure 4.1 on page 63). Even though the rate of turnout decline may have been overestimated[12] the decline is still sizable. Patterson[13] elaborates:

> [2000] was a far cry from the 63 percent turnout for the Kennedy-Nixon race of 1960, which became the benchmark for evaluating participation in subsequent elections. In every presidential election for the next twenty years, turnout fell. It rose by 1 percentage point in 1984, but then dropped 3 points in 1988. Analysts viewed the trend with alarm, but the warning bells really sounded in 1996, when more Americans stayed home than went to the polls on Election Day. In 1960, 68.8 million adults voted and 40.8 million did not. In 1996, 96.3 million came out and 100.2 million passed.
>
> The period from 1960 to 2000 marks the longest ebb in turnout in the nation's history. If in 2000, as in 1960, 63 percent of the electorate had participated, nearly 25 million more people would have voted. If that many queued up at a polling booth in New York City, the line would stretch all the way to Los Angeles and back, twice over.

TRUST IN GOVERNMENT

Trust in government reflects the level of public confidence in the integrity of the government; its adherence to its own moral and ethical principles, and its ability to deliver important services. The level of trust in government expressed by the American people is not what it once was. This is true despite the fact that it has improved significantly since its low point in 1994 (see NES trend-line in Figure 4.2). In response to the question, "How much of the time do you think you can trust the government in Washington to do what is right—just about always, most of the time, or only some of the time?" just 44 percent said "most of the time/just about always" in the year 2000. That put a strong majority—66 percent—in the "only some of the time/never" category. Another comprehensive recent study—a Pew survey conducted in February 1998—put the question in a way that evoked an even more emphatic answer:

> Asked for a simple up-or-down assessment—Would you say you basically trust the federal government in Washington or not?—57 percent say they do not trust the federal government; 39 percent say they do. Favorability ratings elicit almost identical responses—59 percent say they have a very or mostly unfavorable opinion of the federal government; 38 percent say the opposite.[14]

FAITH IN ELECTIONS

Figure 4.3 on page 64 depicts the long-term trend for faith in elections—that is, the belief that elections make the government pay attention to what people think. The National Election Study (NES) has asked the question printed below the Figure 4.3 title every year since 1964. The question focuses on the key function assigned to elections in democratic theory: ensuring the responsiveness of public officials to the preferences of ordinary citizens.[15] Despite the 1992 uptick, the gradual erosion of faith in the electoral process between 1964 and 1988 still leaves it in a diminished state in comparison to its 1964 peak.

INTERPRETATION

The Argument from Results: The System Works   These numbers show that the political system is always on trial, with support and confidence ebbing and flowing with events. But though recent improvements are positive, the long-term trends are downward, raising a fundamental question: Should we be concerned? Not everyone thinks so. Many political scientists argue, for example, that those who express lack of confidence in the government or elections give insufficient weight to the fact that the electoral process actually works quite well.[16] The principal evidence is research showing that election outcomes are primarily determined by substantive factors like national economic and political conditions, rather than by ephemera such as candidate image or manipulative advertising. This effectiveness stems primarily from two sources. First is the success of the major political parties in structuring orderly, policy-relevant competition for office between candidates who usually well-represent their parties' traditional platforms whatever the campaign rhetoric, thereby simplifying the voters' choice of which candidate-party combination best serves their interests.

Second is an electorate that understands partisan cues, is guided by partisan loyalties, yet also "stays focused on a bottom line consisting of peace, prosperity, and moderation"[17] as the basis for voting decisions. The clincher from this angle is that campaigns are seldom as important in determining election outcomes as are voter attributions to parties and candidates of responsibility for the state of the nation. Campaigns, in this view, can make important contributions. But when compared to the record of results, they are distinctly *secondary* contributions, such as informing voters of the state of the nation and the qualifications of the candidates, encouraging citizens to act on the information by voting, stimulating democratic deliberation and communication between citizens and their political leaders, creating a record of public commitment and popular legitimization that may or may not influence the behavior of winning candidates after they take office, and generating and replenishing interest in and support for the political system more generally. While particular election cycles may perform more or less well at delivering these peripheral services, *it is the fact that voters consistently award power on the basis of rational assessment of substantive policy performance that justifies a conclusion that, on the whole, the system works well.* From this perspective, that is what really matters. The additional fact that so many prospective voters are put off or not attracted by the political spectacle, and that many also feel that something is wrong with the process, is admittedly troubling. But such sentiments, while regrettable, are little more than embarrassing to American democratic appearances and pretensions. Many nonparticipants, for example, are merely indifferent, not seriously estranged. And even those who say they hate politics would, for the most part, not dispute the basic legitimacy of American elections, or portray their nonparticipation as a categorical rejection of the American political order.

Rebuttal: The Demands of Democracy On the other side are the critics, including me, who are not reassured by this argument. Many critics believe that citizen disengagement, whether due to disaffection or indifference, is more significant than those who say the system works will allow. The rebuttal begins with the status of voters in the theory of democracy.

Historically important thinkers like Niccolo Machiavelli, James Mill, Jeremy Bentham, and James Madison collectively identify regular elections, secret ballots, and competition for votes as practical ways to promote and protect the people's interests against the abuse that history shows to result from autocratic rule.[18] Similarly, contemporary political theorists like Carole Pateman note that "[e]lections are central to the democratic method because they provide the mechanism through which the control of the leaders by non-leaders can take place."[19] *The control mechanism is the election and reelection incentive, which is supposed to give election candidates compelling reason to take voters' needs and preferences into account.* Political theorist Carl Friedrich[20] called this "*the principle of anticipated reactions.*" Those seeking office anticipate how voters might react to what they propose or do, and take those anticipated reactions into account before taking stands or taking action. This is the root source of the idea that electoral democracy gives voters both the *right* and the *means* to not only decide who the leaders will be, but also to influence what leaders actually do (i.e., *policy*).

· DEMOCRACY DILUTED

In practice, American citizens have not always fully exploited these democratic tools. There are many reasons, but prominent among them is the fact that outside crises, most Americans are sketchily informed at best about the national agenda. That makes it difficult for them to use elections to protect their interests. The problem is compounded when, as in the national elections of 1988 and 1996, or the 2002 midterm elections under way as this was written, candidates seek to manipulate voters by evading or distorting what informed and nonpartisan observers would identify as top policy priorities. In the state of Texas, for example, 2002 candidates for governor attacked each other's faults and swore to avoid tax increases. Ignored were the two top policy problems: how to handle the budget shortfalls that plagued Texas and most other states during the economic downturn, and the related question of how to repair a badly flawed system for financing public education.

Partisan Sniping   The problem is compounded by the uncivil tone of much campaign discourse. Most candidates see issue-oriented attacks and comparisons as a healthy part of the campaign process.[21] But many voters find a steady diet of such fare offensive, particularly when the issues stressed are not voter priorities or high-priority government problems and when mean-spirited *ad hominem* attacks are included. Those most put off by aggressive partisan politics include the least partisan and least well-informed among the electorate—a sizable group. When important substantive concerns do not succeed in overriding the hard edge of the partisan fight, such audiences are reminded once again, as a recent headline put it, that "Invective and Accusations Remain Campaign Staples." This particular headline was prompted when President Bush, defending his Homeland Security bill at a fund-raiser for Republican Congressional candidates, accused opposing Senate Democrats of being more concerned with the political support of labor unions than with the national security of the United States. Most observers thought the president's comment was a low blow, although the story noted that "his campaign trail attack hardly broke new frontiers in American political discourse." But when Tom Daschle, Democratic majority leader of the U.S. Senate, demanded that Bush apologize for impugning the patriotism of Democratic Senators, the ill-will supplanted the policy debate as the headline of the day. The exchange was later described by veteran Republican pollster Robert Teeter as damaging to both men because he knew that many people would not appreciate the descent into meanness. "The public likes the idea of being unified," he said.[22]

Media Complicity   Though the occasional news story takes note of the public's dislike of attack politics, reporters are more likely to treat the attacks rather than the adverse public reaction as news. Typical is a recent conversation I had with a reporter for a national newspaper about the previously-mentioned 2002 Texas Governor's race. I suggested that the candidates' tacit agreement to ignore the central policy question facing the next Texas governor and legislature, a multibillion dollar budget shortfall, showed a striking disregard for the public's need and right to hear them address it. Instead, the combatants were spending millions of dollars on slanderous attack advertising that made no mention of the budget shortfall or any other actual policy problem the next governor would face. His reply: "I just take for granted that what candidates do is not good for the process." He then quickly steered the discussion back to which candidate was helped or hurt the most by the evasions and attacks.

The Costs of Politics

Why are those who say the system works fine just as it is wrong for not paying more attention to public unhappiness with politics? Because, as Walter F. Murphy[23] notes, "for any kind of modern political system to endure and prosper, large numbers of its people must, most of the time, internalize enough of the regime's norms to act willingly and even enthusiastically in general conformity with the most important of these values." Enlightened and purposive voting is just such a value, and many are dissuaded from it by the attack mode of political discourse. If political theorists from Plato to Easton are right in claiming that polities need more than mere tolerance or submission from their citizens to endure and thrive, then the distaste and disengagement of so many citizens, even nonrebellious citizens, is not trivial.

For example, complacent or indifferent as well as negative feelings about politics pose a threat to what David Easton[24] calls "diffuse regime support," which he defines as "a reservoir of favorable attitudes or good will that helps [citizens] to accept or tolerate [government] outputs to which they are opposed." While I include complacency and indifference as well as negativity in my definition of this problem, Easton and others worry more about negative feelings. He, for example, concludes that "if discontent with perceived performance continues over a long enough time, it may gradually erode even the strongest underlying bonds of attachment." Similarly, after reviewing the evidence of discontent, Luttbeg and Gant[25] note that ". . . our findings about change in political trust and alienation do not absolutely refute the notion that contemporary disaffection might render serious damage to our republic." And Stephen Craig[26] after his own survey of the trust, faith in elections, and other discontent data, suggests that: "Even though we do not appear to be on the verge of a full-blown system breakdown, it seems reasonable to conclude that the general health of our polity will continue to deteriorate unless the confidence gap is in some way bridged." To these warnings about outright disaffection I reiterate my proposition that indifference, the "signature" political stance of the young, is no less challenging to the long-term prospects for support.

From this critical perspective, the scope and the quality of the public's support for the electoral process is at least as important as a bottom-line measure of political system health as the government's ability to push the electoral machinery through to a conclusion whatever the level of turnout, or to deliver Social Security checks in the mail. Various systems may in this sense "make the trains run on time." *But authentic representative democracies must also sustain the heartfelt allegiance of the people.* The fact that such a large percentage of the electorate has, for various reasons, walked away from an electoral process that represents history's best effort to equip them to protect their own interests shows clearly that something important is wrong.

AFFIRMATION ATTRACTS VOTERS

That is why it matters whether routine political practice appeals to or offends the sensibilities of ordinary voters. For a quite sizable audience, good campaigns provide a measure of relief from the dispiriting effects of the typical campaign. They will not further repel the estranged by reminding them of what they find objectionable. They are less likely to confirm the indifferent by reminding them of why they don't care. And by featuring issues of real importance, such campaigns can even jostle the complacent, moving some of them to take part.

Good campaigns organize an experience for voters that approximates the core logic of elections in the theory of democracy. And as we see next, repeated approximation of the ideal in practice can in time help to restore trust in government, faith in elections, and voter turnout.

GOOD CAMPAIGNS BUILD REGIME SUPPORT

The third reason why good campaigns matter is because they get greater-than-usual numbers of citizens to invest time and energy, first to learn about the choices they face, and then to vote. I conceive of learning and voting as investment behaviors. As these investments are repeated—election after election—they gradually deepen and strengthen the ties that bind people to the political process. Binding people to the process is important because only an invested citizenry can spearhead the effort to create the healthier national politics envisioned in Chapter 7. For that reason I devote the remainder of this chapter to developing the idea of regime support, and examining evidence that it is encouraged by political participation.

THE CONCEPT OF REGIME SUPPORT

The regime of interest here, of course, is the U.S. political system. For present purposes, I conceive of it primarily in terms of the process that most centrally defines and legitimizes any regime as democratic: national elections. To support a democratic regime is, first and foremost, to support the electoral process. So when I speak of regime support, I mean support by the citizenry of the electoral process. This, after all, is what is called into question by declining turnout and diminished faith in elections. Conversely, voters who believe elections make the government pay attention to what they think are more likely to tolerate what Easton styles as "outputs to which they are opposed" because faith in elections implies the belief that elections can be trusted to make change possible and that individual voters can join to force such change.

Measuring Regime Support

As the indicators in Table 4.1 show, I conceive and operationalize regime support as a *constellation of mutually reinforcing behaviors and attitudes that directly link citizens to the regime via participation in and psychological attachment to its flagship electoral process.* A discussion of the support concepts and indicators follows.

Behaviors

The Significance of Voting   The larger significance of the act of voting is nicely captured by Riker:[27]

> . . . all democratic ideas are focused on the mechanism of voting. All the elements of the democratic method are means to render voting practically effective and politically significant, and all the elements of the democratic ideal are moral extensions and elaborations of the features of the method that make voting work. Voting, therefore, is the central act of democracy. . . .

More directly to the point here, voting (and attitudes that encourage it) indicate regime support because a high incidence of voting confers legitimacy on a representative democracy.

Table 4.1   Regime Supportive Behavior and Attitudes in Presidential Elections

	1988	1992	1996
Behavior			
Voter Turnout[1]	50.1%	55.2%	48.8%
Issue Knowledge[2]	4	7	1
Attitudes[3]			
Voting is very important to me.	77%	73%	72%
I am very interested in presidential politics.	37	42	35
Citizen duty: Vote/register to vote[4]			70
Citizen duty: Stay informed/ maintain political awareness[4]			25

[1]Federal Election Commission.

[2]Number of issue positions attributed to candidates correctly by 58%+ of respondents, on a 20-item issue position test.

[3]Sources: 1988, Louis Harris & Associates, 10/18–11/4/1988, n = 1,875; 1992, Princeton Survey Research Associates, 10/20–11/2/1992, n = 1,882; 1996, PSRA, 10/21–11/2/1996, n = 1,881.

[4]Source: PSRA, 1996 only, 10/21/1996, n = 945. What are the most important responsibilities that citizens have during a presidential election year?

The Significance of Learning and Knowledge   Like the duty to vote, the normative ideal of a well-informed electorate is a fixture of the democratic tradition. As Rousseau put it in *The Social Contract:* "Born as I was the citizen of a free state and a member of its sovereign body, the very right to vote imposes on me the duty to instruct myself in public affairs, however little influence my voice may have in them."[28] American Democratic theorists from Thomas Jefferson to John Dewey to Walter Lippmann to Amy Gutmann and Dennis Thompson have pointed to the informed citizenry ideal while acknowledging that it is rarely achieved and proposing various ways to compensate for the shortfall.

There are many reasons to regard learning and knowledge as important for civic self-protection and regime enhancement.[29] But the key feature of learning stressed for present purposes is its potential as one of two key forms of effortful behavioral investment (the other is voting) likely to nurture supportive attitudes.

The learning portion of the civic investment model subsequently described and illustrated with data uses a three-campaign series of twenty-item issue position test data from the Markle campaign surveys (Table 4.1 on page 71 and Table 4.4 on page 77). Item characterizations are in Chapter 5, Table 5.3.

ATTITUDES

Instilling and sustaining the psychological allegiance of citizens to regimes, as of members to any social organization, is fundamental to system health and survival and thus necessarily a core objective of system maintenance.[30] No measures of citizen-regime bonding or regime-supportive attitudes known to me fully encompasses all the potentially important dimensions of commitment or allegiance of citizens to the regime.[31] But while they obviously do not exhaust the concept, the three attitudinal indicators in Table 4.1—voting importance, political interest, and an open-ended question on citizen duty—clearly tap important dimensions of regime support.

Political interest measures the motivation to pay attention to the campaign. It (and associated practices like following media coverage and discussing the campaign with others) is, in other words, both the initial hook and the sustaining force, without which learning and voting are far less likely. In the Markle series, interest is measured by the question, "How interested are you in presidential politics?" The *Voting Importance* question, "How important is voting in the November presidential election to you?" taps the extent to which respondents profess that the core regime-supportive act is a personal priority, and thus, by implication, a component of self-definition. *Citizen Duty* is an open-ended question: "Now, please think about the responsibilities and duties of being a U.S. citizen. In your opinion, what are the most important responsibilities that citizens have during a presidential election year? Are there any other important responsibilities that citizens have? Responses to this question, posed to Markle national samples for the first and only time in 1996, show what political socialization has instilled in the mass public mind regarding citizens' presidential election year responsibilities. Registering and voting dominate the self-defined citizen portfolio at 70 percent, with watching and learning a distant second at 25 percent.

LEARNING AND VOTING AS INVESTMENT BEHAVIORS

My argument in the previous section of this chapter was that citizen exposure to the positive and substantive focus of good campaigns helps to *counteract feelings of political indifference and disaffection*. With the concept of regime support now before us, the next piece of the argument can be presented. It is that as participation becomes habitual, it *works to strengthen the ties that bind: namely, regime support*. The reason, as a respected body of social-psychological research has shown, is that the best way to encourage any *attitude* is by inspiring *behavior* that reinforces it.

Effortful behavior, such as learning and voting, tends, when the behavior is regularly repeated and socially reinforced, to solidify or *freeze* attitudes that are consistent with the behavior, such as the personal importance of learning and voting, or the belief that faith in elections is justified. One body of supportive theory and research comes from the cognitive consistency and behavior commitment schools of psychology. The basic idea can be expressed succinctly: "Behavior, if explicit enough, freezes one, in Lewin's terms. Explicit behavior, like an irrevocable decision, provides the pillar around which the cognitive apparatus must be draped. Through behavior, one is *committed*."[32] Normative political theorists have advanced a similar proposition: that civic participation promotes satisfaction with the polity and makes the individual more likely to consider the institutions, norms, and values of a given regime morally proper.[33] International comparisons suggest that participation increases the tendency to view any political regime as legitimate and increases the acceptability of collective decisions and policy outcomes.[34]

EVIDENCE FROM CAMPAIGNS

There is scattered evidence that political campaigns, both good and bad, encourage attitudes supportive of the political system *among citizens who take part*. There are indications, for example, that participation in the 1968 and 1972 presidential elections mobilized citizen support for the regime and for political leaders.[35] More recently, Rahn and her colleagues[36] found that the 1992 presidential election positively affected both economic expectations and trust in government among a small sample of Madison, Wisconsin, residents. They also cite other evidence suggesting the role of elections in elevating peoples' spirits, including the impact of optimistic election rhetoric on "the spirit of community." A particularly ambitious look at the

1996 election tested the ability of four classes of campaign exposure—mobilization, campaign involvement, perceived qualities of the campaign and candidates, and the election ritual—to explain changes in three interrelated attitudes that represent "the core normative apparatus of democracy." The attitudes were generalized trust in others, trust in government, and "external political efficacy" (defined as the belief that the political authorities are responsive to citizen demands). The researchers found that parts of each campaign exposure had significant impacts on the attitudes. For example, one aspect of mobilization—being contacted by a political party—had a modest positive impact on social trust. One aspect of campaign involvement—voting—clearly boosted respondents' feelings of political efficacy. Those who perceived "multiple positive aspects" about both presidential candidates, Bill Clinton and Bob Dole, expressed more trust in government after than before the election. And exposure to the election ritual increased social trust. This was especially pronounced among those who were the most politically knowledgeable and active at the start. But the increase was also apparent among many who initially expressed high levels of distrust.[37]

Another study (see Table 4.2) found that exposure to the 1988, 1992, and 1996 campaigns (which in practical terms means exposure to media coverage, campaign advertising, and face-to-face exchanges with friends, associates, and neighbors about the campaign, issues, and candidates) sparked an increase in the average level of reported interest in the contest and also an increase in the percentage of the eligible electorate that followed media coverage of the campaign "very closely." Again, interest and media attention matter because campaigns and elections cannot influence behavior like learning and voting without first attracting attention.

TABLE 4.2   CAMPAIGN INFLUENCE ON REGIME-SUPPORTIVE ATTITUDES

	1988[1]		1992[2]		1996[3]	
	(1)	(2)	(1)	(2)	(1)	(2)
Voting is important to me[4]	8.9	9.1	8.6	8.8	8.5	8.8
Voting is a citizen duty[5]					60%	70%
I am interested in politics[4]	7.1	7.4	7.1	7.5	6.9	7.1
I follow media very closely	16%	25%	22%	38%	20%	24%

[1]Louis Harris & Associates survey 1988: (1) n = 1,876, conducted 9/6–9/19/1988; (2) n = 1,875, conducted 10/18–11/4/1988.

[2]Princeton Survey Research Associates survey 1992: (1) n = 1,882, conducted 9/8–9/21/1992; (2) n = 1,882, conducted 10/20–11/2/1992.

[3]PSRA survey 1996: (1) n = 1,923, conducted 9/6–9/16/1996; (2) n = 1,881, conducted 10/21–11/2/1996.

[4]Means on scales of 1 to 10, with 10 being highest.

[5]Open-ended question, 1996 only: "Now, thinking about the responsibilities and duties of being a U.S. citizen. In your opinion, what are the MOST important responsibilities that citizens have during a presidential election year?"

Exposure to each of these campaigns also appears to have sparked modest increases in reported "personal importance of voting." And in 1996, the only year in which this particular open-ended, citizen-duty question was asked, the percent of respondents that identified voting as the most important civic responsibility during a presidential election year moved from 60 to 70 between Labor Day and Election Day.[38]

ATTITUDES AND BEHAVIOR: RECIPROCAL EFFECTS

These studies show that participation affects various expressions of regime-supportive attitudes. There is also evidence that voting behavior and regime-supportive attitudes reinforce and strengthen each other over time. Finkel,[39] for example, tested the proposition that reciprocal causation exists between external efficacy and electoral participation. He found that the individual who votes or participates develops stronger feelings that the government is responsive, which then makes future participation more likely. Nonparticipation, on the other hand, reinforces the sense that the government is unresponsive, which discourages participation. Finkel also finds evidence of directional influence between voting and external efficacy throughout his large sample but especially among less educated citizens, a low turnout group. Separate studies of both U.S. and German voters led this investigator to conclude that the impact of voting on supportive attitudes "may be a very general process in western democracies."

The hypothesis that learning, like voting, is a form of investment behavior with attitudinal consequences of its own has received less direct research attention. Most relevant studies focus on the relationship of participation and education, learning or knowledge, and do not consider learning variables as potential predictors of supportive attitudes. But in their review of studies[40] showing the strong relationship between participation and knowledge, Delli Carpini and Keeter[41] observe that "Knowledge promotes a number of civic attitudes . . . (such as political interest and efficacy) that motivate participation," and conclude that knowledge boosts participation *because it promotes an understanding of why politics is relevant.* The "knowledge = increased respect for politics = participation" model implicit in their argument is essentially the same "behavior-attitude-behavior" reinforcement dynamic postulated here, and it is also implied by the relationships reported in the next two tables.

EVIDENCE

The percentage comparisons reported in Tables 4.3 and 4.4 show that *people who report stronger regime-supportive attitudes are more likely to behave supportively* (i.e., to report having registered and voted and to demonstrate greater learning). Table 4.3 (on page 76) shows that significantly greater percentages of those who express interest in presidential politics and attach importance

TABLE 4.3   IMPACT OF INTEREST AND IMPORTANCE
ON VOTING AND VOTER REGISTRATION

How interested are you in presidential politics? Use a 10 to 1 scale where 10 means you
are VERY INTERESTED and 1 means you are NOT INTERESTED.

	TOTAL INTERESTED (6–10)	TOTAL NOT INTERESTED (1–4)	VERY INTERESTED (9–10)	NEUTRAL (5)	NOT INTERESTED (1–2)
Who Voted	81%	51%	86%	54%	52%
Who Didn't Vote	19	49	14	45	48
Registered	89	61	92	68	57
Not Registered	11	39	8	32	43

How important is voting in the November presidential election to you? Use a 10 to 1
scale where 10 means VERY IMPORTANT to you and 1 means NOT IMPORTANT to you.

	TOTAL IMPORTANT (6–10)	TOTAL NOT IMPORTANT (1–4)	VERY IMPORTANT (9–10)	NEUTRAL (5)	NOT IMPORTANT (1–2)
Who Voted	78%	31%	82%	42%	32%
Who Didn't Vote	22	69	18	58	68
Registered	86	44	90	58	46
Not Registered	14	56	10	42	54

Source: Princeton Survey Research Associates, 10/21–11/2/1996.

to voting (indicated by ratings between six and ten on a ten-point scale) *claim to have voted in 1992 and to have registered in 1996* than do those who express no interest (indicated by ratings between one and four). Table 4.3 shows that people who claim to have voted in 1992 and to have registered in 1996 attach significantly greater importance to voting and express significantly greater interest in presidential politics—two regime-supportive attitudes—than do self-described nonvoters and nonregistrants. The table also shows that similar, equally significant differences between voters and nonvoters emerge in responses to the open-ended citizen duty question.

By the same token, Table 4.4 shows that *those expressing higher levels of political interest and ascribing more importance to voting demonstrate more learning* on the issues test than those who report less interest and attach less importance. For example, the "very important" and "very interested" respondents are more than two and three times as likely, respectively, than the "not at all important, not at all interested" respondents to score in the high-knowledge category. On a related note, 70 percent of those who said that citizens should

TABLE 4.4 IMPACT OF INTEREST AND IMPORTANCE ON KNOWLEDGE

How interested are you in presidential politics? Use a 10 to 1 scale where 10 means you are VERY INTERESTED and 1 means you are NOT INTERESTED.

	TOTAL INTERESTED (6–10)	TOTAL NOT INTERESTED (1–4)	VERY INTERESTED (9–10)	NEUTRAL (5)	NOT INTERESTED (1–2)
Knowledge Index					
Scoring High	24%	11%	28%	8%	8%
Scoring Medium	39	30	41	39	30
Scoring Low	37	59	31	53	62

How important is voting in the November presidential election to you? Use a 10 to 1 scale where 10 means VERY IMPORTANT to you and 1 means NOT IMPORTANT to you.

	TOTAL IMPORTANT (6–10)	TOTAL NOT IMPORTANT (1–4)	VERY IMPORTANT (9–10)	NEUTRAL (5)	NOT IMPORTANT (1–2)
Knowledge Index					
Scoring High	21%	9%	23%	13%	10%
Scoring Medium	38	41	38	32	43
Scoring Low	41	50	39	54	47

Source: Princeton Survey Research Associates, 10/21–11/2/1996.

"stay informed and maintain political awareness" in response to the open-ended, citizen-duty question scored in the high or medium knowledge categories, while only 30 percent achieved low-knowledge scores (not reported in tables). And the low-supportive-attitude groups are significantly more likely to score in the low-knowledge category.

These results add to the weight of available evidence showing a strong positive association between political attitudes and related behavior. Much of it[42] also demonstrates reciprocal causal effects between attitudinal and behavioral variables. It is reasonable to conclude, therefore, that regime-supportive attitudes and behavior are mutually reinforcing

SUMMARY: LEARNING AND VOTING INCREASE SUPPORT

The evidence is clear. It shows that there is *no better estrangement-or-indifference-reduction vehicle available than a national election campaign.* Such campaigns offer something that cannot be found anywhere else in national civic life: a regularly scheduled opportunity for support-affirming behavior on a mass scale. Campaigns that are able, like 1992's, to induce more people than usual to learn and vote (see Table 4.1 on page 71) have a greater capacity than less influential campaigns to reinforce pro-voting and pro-learning attitudes that are intrinsically regime-enhancing and supportive. Given the evidence of a reciprocal link between attitudes and behavior, several such campaigns in succession should significantly improve the trend-lines on such regime support variables as trust in government, faith in elections, and a belief in the personal importance of voting.

CONCLUSION

Finally, let me bring this chapter to a close by suggesting the meaning of the relationships among the three propositions I used to organize it. Good campaigns contribute to the health of the polity by affirming democratic values and reinforcing voter allegiance. These can be regarded as normative benefits. But the higher levels of participation and greater focus on issues that such campaigns foster also help to mobilize and legitimize solutions to national problems. This is a decidedly practical benefit.

It is noteworthy that citizens are implicated in both kinds of payoffs, first as beneficiaries and then as contributors. There is, in fact, an implicit *quid pro quo*: respect and useful information for prospective voters in return for their legitimizing participation. The alternative is the *status quo* campaign that adds little to system vitality because it engages many fewer people and does not address high-priority problems.

By now it should be clear that nurturing good campaigns can be a viable strategy for strengthening the American political system. It makes sense to do what is necessary to attract and sustain citizen participation at levels that both reinforce democracy and strengthen problem-solving capacity. The problem, which should also be clear, is *how to find causes more orderly than crises to set and keep the good campaign dynamic in motion.* My proposal, detailed in Chapter 7, is to supplement unpredictable crises with the gradual cultivation of an invested citizenry as the mainspring of high-quality presidential campaigns.

Before we get to that, however, two prior questions require attention. The first, addressed in the next chapter, focuses on the policy side of the equation. How do elections actually influence policy? If substantive campaigns followed by high voter turnout increase the likelihood of an impact on the choice of policy, how does that impact actually unfold?

NOTES

1. Bernard R. Berelson, Paul F. Lazarsfeld, and William N. McPhee, *Voting* (Chicago: University of Chicago Press, 1954).
2. Robert A. Dahl, *A Preface to Democratic Theory* (Chicago: University of Chicago Press, 1956).

3. Steven J. Rosenstone and John Mark Hansen, *Mobilization, Participation, and Democracy in America* (New York: Macmillan, 1993), p. 150.

4. Ruy A. Teixeira, *The Disappearing American Voter* (Washington, D.C.: Brookings, 1992), p. 3.

5. James Robert Sharp, *American Politics in the Early Republic: The New Nation in Crisis* (New Haven, CT: Yale University Press, 1993), p. 119.

6. Ibid., pp. 5–8.

7. Ibid., p. 274.

8. Gil Troy, *See How They Ran: The Changing Role of the Presidential Candidate* (New York: Free Press, 1991), pp. 18, 86.

9. Charles O. Jones, *The Presidency in a Separated System* (Washington, D.C.: Brookings, 1994), p. 149.

10. Thomas E. Patterson, *The Vanishing Voter: Public Involvement in an Age of Uncertainty* (New York: Knopf, 2002), quotation from Chapter 1 excerpt, <randomhouse.com> Web site.

11. Cf., Larry M. Bartels, "Campaign Quality: Standards for Evaluation, Benchmarks for Reform," in *Campaign Reform: Insights and Evidence*, ed. Larry M. Bartels and Lynn Vavreck (Ann Arbor, MI: University of Michigan Press, 2000); James D. Hunter and Daniel C. Johnson, "A State of Disunion?" *Public Perspective* 8 (1997), pp. 35–38; John R. Hibbing and Elizabeth Theiss-Morse, *Congress as Public Enemy* (New York: Cambridge University Press, 1995); Norman R. Luttbeg and Michael M. Gant, *American Electoral Behavior, 1952–1992*, 2nd ed. (Itasca, IL: Peacock, 1995); Stephen C. Craig, *The Malevolent Leaders: Popular Discontent in America* (Boulder, CO: Westview, 1993); Seymour M. Lipset and William Schneider, *The Confidence Gap*, rev. ed. (Baltimore, MD: Johns Hopkins University Press, 1987); Arthur H. Miller, "Political Issues and Trust in Government: 1964–1970," *American Political Science Review* 68 (1974), pp. 951–972.

12. Michael P. McDonald and Samuel L. Popkin, "The Myth of the Vanishing Vote," *American Political Science Review* 95 (2001), pp. 963–974.

13. Thomas E. Patterson, *The Vanishing Voter: Public Involvement in an Age of Uncertainty* (New York: Knopf, 2002), quotation from Chapter 1 excerpt, <randomhouse.com> Web site.

14. Pew Research Center for the People and the Press, "Deconstructing Distrust: How Americans View Government" (Washington, D.C.: 1998).

15. Larry M. Bartels, "Question Order and Declining Faith in Elections," *Public Opinion Quarterly* 66 (2002), pp. 67–79.

16. Larry M. Bartels and Lynn Vavrek, eds., *Campaign Reform: Insights and Evidence* (Ann Arbor, MI: University of Michigan Press, 2000).

17. John R. Zaller, "Monica Lewinsky's Contribution to Political Science," *PS: Political Science and Politics* 31 (1998), pp. 182–189.

18. David Held, *Models of Democracy*, 2nd ed. (Stanford, CA: Stanford University Press, 1996), p. 44.

19. Carole Pateman, *Participation and Democratic Theory* (Cambridge: Cambridge University Press, 1970), p. 8.

20. Carl Friedrich, *Constitutional Government and Democracy*, 2nd ed. (Boston: Ginn, 1941).

21. Allen Churchill, "The Zest to Serve and the Opportunity to Engage," in *Campaign Battle Lines*, ed. Ronald A. Faucheux and Paul S. Herrnson (Washington, D.C.: Campaigns and Elections Publishing Co., 2002), pp. 325–331.

22. Adam Clymer, "Invective and Accusations Remain Campaign Staples," *New York Times*, 29 September 2002, p. 13.

23. Walter F. Murphy, "Creating Citizens for a Constitutional Democracy" (unpublished manuscript, Princeton University, 1994).

24. David Easton, "A Re-Assessment of the Concept of Political Support," *British Journal of Political Science* 5 (1975), pp. 444–445.

25. Norman R. Luttbeg and Michael M. Gant, *American Electoral Behavior, 1952–1992*, 2nd ed. (Itasca, IL: Peacock, 1995), p. 162.

26. Stephen C. Craig, *The Malevolent Leaders: Popular Discontent in America* (Boulder, CO: Westview, 1993), p. 17.

27. William H. Riker, *Liberalism against Populism* (Prospect Heights, IL: Waveland Press, 1982), p. 6.

28. Jean-Jacques Rousseau, *The Social Contract* (London: Penguin Books, 1968), p. 49.

29. cf., Norman H. Nie, Jane Junn, and Kenneth Stehlik-Barry, *Education and Democratic Citizenship in America* (Chicago, IL: University of Chicago Press, 1996); Michael X. Delli Carpini,

and Scott Keeter, *What Americans Know about Politics and Why It Matters* (New Haven, CT: Yale University Press, 1996).

30. David Easton, *A Systems Analysis of Political Life* (New York: Wiley, 1965); Joseph Katz and Robert Kahn, *The Social Psychology of Organizations*, 2nd ed. (New York: Wiley, 1978); Bruce Buchanan, "Building Organizational Commitment," *Administrative Science Quarterly* 19 (1974), pp. 533–546.

31. Cf., Ronald Beiner, ed., *Theorizing Citizenship* (Albany, NY: State University of New York Press, 1995).

32. Charles A. Kiesler, *The Psychology of Commitment: Experiments Linking Behavior to Belief* (New York: Academic Press, 1971), p. 17.

33. See, for example, Dennis Thompson, *The Democratic Citizen* (Cambridge, England: Cambridge University Press, 1970).

34. Sidney Verba, *Small Groups and Political Behavior* (Princeton, NJ: Princeton University Press, 1961); Gabriel Almond and Sidney Verba, *The Civic Culture* (Princeton, NJ: Princeton University Press, 1963).

35. Benjamin Ginsberg and R. Weissberg, "Elections and the Mobilization of Popular Support," *American Journal of Political Science* 22 (1978), pp. 31–55; Harold D. Clark and Alan C. Acock, "National Elections and Political Attitudes: The Case of Political Efficacy," *British Journal of Political Science* 19 (1989), pp. 551–562.

36. Wendy M. Rahn et al., "The Etiology and Attitudinal Consequences of the Public's Mood" (paper presented at the annual meeting of the International Society of Political Psychology, San Francisco, 1993).

37. Wendy M. Rahn, John Brehm, and Neil Carlson, "National Elections as Institutions for Generating Social Capital" (paper presented at the annual meeting of the American Political Science Association, Washington, D.C., 1997).

38. In Table 4.2, the campaign season (i.e., time 1–time 2) comparisons within each election year, though based on separate random national samples for each September–November comparison (multiple cross-sections) reveal differences that are plausibly interpreted as changes brought on by exposure to the campaign. While the magnitude of the changes varies from year to year, all show increases from September to November. The very large sample sizes in the table ensure that all mean differences are statistically significant.

39. Steven E. Finkel, "Reciprocal Effects of Participation and Political Efficacy: A Panel Analysis," *American Journal of Political Science* 29 (1985), pp. 891–913.

40. See, for example, Jane Junn, "Participation and Political Knowledge," in *Political Participation and American Democracy*, ed. William Crotty (New York: Greenwood Press, 1991); Jan Leighley, "Participation as a Stimulus of Political Conceptualization," *Journal of Politics* 53 (1991), pp. 198–211, and others.

41. Michael X. Delli Carpini and Scott Keeter, *What Americans Know about Politics and Why It Matters* (New Haven, CT: Yale University Press, 1996), p. 224.

42. Jan Leighley, "Participation as a Stimulus of Political Conceptualization," *Journal of Politics* 53 (1991), pp. 198–211; Steven E. Finkel, "Reciprocal Effects of Participation and Political Efficacy: A Panel Analysis," *American Journal of Political Science* 29 (1985), pp. 891–913; Steven E. Finkel, "The Effects of Participation on Political Efficacy and Political Support: Evidence from a West German Panel," *Journal of Politics* 49 (1987), pp. 441–464.

BEYOND MANDATES

THE POLICY SIGNAL

The time has come to distinguish the kinds of impacts a presidential campaign can have on policy after an election, and to assess the role that voters play in the creation of such impacts. I will again use evidence from the Markle election studies and other surveys, plus occasional references to the cases reviewed earlier and to other relevant campaign history, to distinguish what I call *policy signals* from the more conventional idea of a policy mandate.

POLICY MANDATES

The idea of a policy mandate as the product of a victorious presidential election campaign was once enshrined as accepted "responsible party" doctrine. Proponent E. E. Schattschneider,[1] for whom the central democratic question was "how can the people get control of the government?" conceived the answer to require competing parties and candidates to define the alternatives of public policy crisply and clearly enough so that by electing a particular candidate, voters also endorsed a specific policy agenda. Increasingly complex national problems, such as how to maintain the health of the economy and how best to define the role of the United States in world affairs, demanded attentive citizens willing to seek out the best policies, not just for themselves, but for the nation as a whole. This, in Schattschneider's view, was democracy's bottom line. Only a nationally oriented citizenry equipped to grant specific policy mandates in national elections could make voters sovereign in fact as well as in theory.

More recently, close students of electoral politics have questioned whether authentic policy mandates can ever be achieved in practice. One critic, for example, contends that mandates are impossible to measure, given the difficulty of sorting out a clear picture of the policy intentions of millions of voters.[2] As Polsby and Wildavsky note, "voters in presidential elections do not transmit their policy preferences to elected officials with a high degree of reliability."[3] Further, candidates add additional confusion by proposing contradictory policies to different constituencies. Thus, Bill Clinton in 1992 promised both to reduce health care costs and to provide universal coverage; to ensure that the United States kept its position of world leadership but also to reduce U.S. military presence abroad; to protect American jobs, but also to promote free trade and strict environmental regulations.[4] Presidents do often claim, and under certain circumstances get, credit from Congress and media for policy mandates.[5] But that is usually a measure of successful elite bargaining and political persuasion, not of the voters' conscious intent that the election winner should push a specific course of action.[6]

On the other hand, few would dispute what realignment scholars and others commonly assert: that some presidential elections have extraordinarily significant policy consequences. Obvious examples include the elections of 1860, which prefigured the Civil War; 1896, which installed the Republican tariff and other pro-business policies; and 1932, which signaled the rise of the New Deal. Other campaigns and elections, such as those of 1960, 1964, 1980, 1992, and 2000 may not have reordered the political or policy universe on quite so grand a scale. But they did contribute to important changes in Soviet relations, civil rights, tax law, budget priorities, and foreign policy, respectively.

The question, then, is how best to conceive and measure the most important policy consequences of presidential campaigns and elections. I will make the case that most of the problems raised by mandate critics can be avoided, and the significant policy implications of campaigns and elections clarified, through the use of the related but less restrictive idea of a "policy signal."

POLICY SIGNALS

In the broadest sense, virtually every presidential election has policy consequences at some level, if only because the winner will have opportunities denied the loser to influence the national agenda in ways large and small. Had Michael Dukakis won in 1988, for example, he would not have embraced the pro-life position on abortion, as George Bush did. And had Bush won in 1992, he would not have pressed the Earned Income Tax Credit, as Bill Clinton did. Whether mentioned during the campaign or not, such things are certainly policy consequences resulting from the election victories of particular candidates. But they are not policy signals.

As I conceive and measure them here, policy signals are election related, and they involve the big picture. They reflect the potential of campaigns to forge a consensus that certain policy problems are to be considered top national priorities. They also reflect the potential of campaigns to help generate the political will to address such big problems. For these reasons, the policy signal concept incorporates only the issues that get the most attention and the highest billing from the major players in the electoral triangle as the campaign nears Election Day.

Excluded are policy problems not regarded as top priorities by national majorities of those eligible to vote. Excluded too is policy influence, however significant, initiated after the election that has little or no anchor in the campaign.

DEFINITION AND MEASUREMENT

I conceive a policy signal to include three components: first, a crystallization of national priorities, evidenced by a broad preelection consensus that some problem or problem-set deserves the immediate attention of the government; second, plausible evidence to suggest that the election ratified the consensus and created some measure of policy momentum; and third, evidence that a postelection attempt is made to take action.

Two points worth clarifying involve consensus and action. First, the consensus that helps to create momentum for action may be either an agreement simply to address the problem, with the means for addressing it left unspecified (e.g., the United States must marshal its resources to win the Cold War; the deficit must somehow be reduced) or the consensus might be to attack the problem in a specific way (e.g., more and larger ICBMs will give the United States the necessary edge over the Soviet Union; the deficit will be reduced with a combination of gasoline tax increases and reductions in Medicare and Social Security spending). Either way, a true consensus will have created an authoritative signal to the incoming leadership that action on some problem must be a high priority.

Second, requiring evidence of postelection action is warranted because that completes the policy signal (in the sense of bringing it to postelection closure) while also retroactively validating the signal's preelection stages. But whether the action actually "succeeds" or not (i.e., gets enacted into law, and/or produces an intended result) is excluded from the definitional test because electoral momentum is but one of many variables able to influence ultimate success and failure. The policy signal indicators are listed in Table 5.1 on page 84. Let us consider them in relation to each component.

CONVERGENT PRIORITIES

The first component, to repeat, is a campaign crystallization of national priorities, evidenced by a broad consensus among candidates, potential voters, and the news media, that some problem or problem-set deserves the immediate attention of the government. National political campaigns traditionally give rise to questions about the national agenda, and one important indication of a consensus is the extent of campaign-season convergence of opinion among

TABLE 5.1   POLICY SIGNAL INDICATORS

Preelection Policy Consensus

Voter-identified "most important problems"

Problems attracting most media stories

Candidate responsiveness to voter priorities

Ratification and Policy Momentum

Number of candidate positions responsive to voter priorities

Postelection Policy Action

Legislative/nonlegislative action responsive to voter priorities and candidate proposals

---

the major players on the identity of "the most important problems" as the election approaches.

The top two policy priorities of candidates, media, and voters for three of the four campaigns examined in Chapters 2 and 3, 1988, 1992, and 1996, appear in Table 5.2. Evidence of the mass public's policy priorities in 1960 was introduced in Chapter 2. Coding studies of media coverage patterns and evidence of candidate policy priorities for the 1960 campaign, which preceded

TABLE 5.2   POLICY PRIORITIES, CANDIDATES, MEDIA, AND VOTERS
(1988, 1992, AND 1996 PRESIDENTIAL CAMPAIGNS)

	1988	1992	1996
Candidates[1]			
	25%	55%	30%
	(N = 5)	(N = 11)	(N = 6)
Media[2]			
	domestic policy	economic policy	taxes
	economic policy	domestic policy	economic policy
Voters[3]			
	deficit (23%)	economy/jobs (48%)	economy/jobs (19%)
	drug traffic (21%)	deficit (31%)	deficit (15%)

[1]Percentage of twenty candidate proposals responsive to the two most important national problems as identified by voters.

[2]Top two policy story categories as shown by print/broadcast content analysis, September through November, for each election year. 1988: Luce Press Clipping Service; 1992 and 1996: Center for Media and Public Affairs.

[3]Voters' priorities from telephone surveys in late October of each election year. Sources: 1988: Louis Harris and Associates; 1992 and 1996: Princeton Survey Research Associates.

the initial Markle study by twenty-eight years, either do not exist or are not precisely comparable to the Markle data reported in tables. Consequently, when discussing 1960 candidate and media priorities, I rely on inferences from the record summarized in Chapter 2.

Voter, candidate, and media priorities are each measured differently in Table 5.2. Those of *prospective voters* reflect answers to direct questions about their priorities taken from pre–Election Day surveys. *Media* coverage priorities are measured by the total number of stories devoted to particular policy categories between Labor Day and Election Day, on the assumption that the more stories devoted to a policy topic, the higher the priority attached to conveying information about that topic. And for reasons best explained after the introduction of additional data later, *candidate* priorities are measured by the percentage of the twenty most prominent issue positions and proposals of the leading candidates in each year that is consistent with (responsive to) the top-two voter priorities for that year.

Findings   Table 5.2 shows that there *was more of a convergence on priorities in 1992 than in 1988 or 1996.* Candidates made more proposals that were responsive to the top national problems identified by voters in that year. In 1992, media coverage was similarly convergent in its emphasis on voters' economic priorities. And it is very likely that convergence was greatest in 1992 because the voters' consensus was so much larger in that than in either other year. The table shows that fully 79 percent of survey respondents agreed on the primacy of the interrelated problem-set of the economy, jobs, and the deficit. By the same logic, the Gallup and Pool et al. poll evidence cited in Chapter 2 (Table 2.1, page 26) showing that large majorities of 1960s prospective voters were anxious about the risk of nuclear war, and considered foreign policy, and particularly Soviet relations, to be "the most important problem facing the country today," pushed candidates and media to emphasize those topics. Clearly, the intensive media focus on candidate issue arguments in 1960 could not have avoided featuring such topics as the missile gap alleged by Kennedy, along with his plans to confront Soviet expansionism. That both candidates generated a flurry of related proposals is evident in Richard Nixon's own detailed summary of his most important 1960 policy positions in his book *Six Crises.* My informal count shows that some 60 percent of them dealt with Soviet relations and military preparedness.[7]

What Sets Priorities   What determines the priorities of each group of actors? The interaction of context and incentives. Consider voters first. When large majorities agree on the urgency of a small handful of economic problems, as in 1992, many clearly get their sense of urgency from anxious reaction to their own experience (e.g., unemployment, rising prices) or empathetic reaction to the experience of others like themselves whom they know or hear about. In 1960, personal anxiety about the possibility of nuclear war with the

Soviet Union was palpable, as suggested by the 71 percent in favor of a law requiring local communities to build bomb shelters.[8] In such circumstances, candidates and media will be hard pressed to change the subject. Their influence will be limited either to reinforcing what voters already feel, or trying to shape the ways citizens interpret and vote on what they feel.

In campaign years not driven by alarm, there is no majority consensus on priorities. Instead, we get single-digit clusters supporting many different policy priorities, as in 1988 or 1996. In such years, the potential of candidates and media to influence the policy agenda expands. In 1988, for example, both major candidates avoided substantial discussion of the deficit. This attracted a certain amount of high-profile media attention to the fact that the candidates were ducking the issue, as well as to the importance of the deficit problem itself. In early September, only about 18 percent identified the deficit as a high priority. But by early November, the number had increased to twenty-three percent.[9] Given the candidates' evasion of the issue, this modest increase was clearly the result of the media attention. In that same year, drugs floated to the top of a long list of small-percentage voter priorities in part because of the well-publicized attention given the issue by candidate Jesse Jackson throughout the primary season and in part because of the highly publicized drug-related indictment of Gen. Manuel Antonio Noriega, the former Panamanian dictator. We saw in Chapter 2 that candidate Kennedy managed to intensify peoples' economic concerns. But he was able to do so in part because sluggish growth, an uptick in unemployment, and problems in the farming sector all bespoke a latent popular readiness to respond. Thus, voter priorities can be influenced by both media and candidates. But as these examples also suggest, neither candidates nor media is likely to exert more than modest influence at the margins. They are extremely unlikely, for example, to be influential enough to "create," without the help of some degree of pre-existing sentiment, a durable majority consensus that a particular problem deserves the next president's immediate attention. There is substantial evidence to suggest that neither candidates nor presidents have much luck swaying the masses to endorse their priorities.[10] The 1960 and 1992 cases in particular suggest that a strong majority consensus is much more likely to evolve out of alarmed reactions to events, such as bad economic news or international turbulence, than out of the campaign strategies of politicians. Neither candidates nor media can expect to create durable public urgency where it did not previously exist. Even in crisis, these actors are not initiators but responders, exploiters, and amplifiers, trumpeting and reporting such events as the Sputnik launch or unemployment statistics. When real news sparks unusual public attention, politicians and reporters react, helping to reinforce and spread the alarm.

Media policy coverage priorities are most often a function of the emergence of particular issues as a topic of discussion by candidates during the campaign. Candidate attention is what makes an issue newsworthy, and thus deserving of coverage. In 1988, for example, a spate of campaign season stories about toxic waste was stimulated by the Bush campaign's "Boston Harbor pollution" ads and related attacks on Michael Dukakis.[11] While most 1992 coverage dealt with the economy, several in-depth analyses of the health care system were prompted by Clinton health care reform proposals.[12] Similarly, the dominance of taxes as a story category in 1996 stemmed from Steve Forbes' emphasis on taxes in the primaries, and Bob Dole's continuation of that emphasis in the fall campaign.[13] Dole also stressed deficit reduction, and primary candidate Pat Buchanan emphasized trade policy. These candidate emphases made the deficit and trade priority media coverage topics during the primary season in particular. And in the run-up to the 2000 election, Democratic candidate Bill Bradley proposed a comprehensive health care package, generating a national discussion and high-profile media attention to the prospect of comprehensive health care reform most observers thought highly unlikely so soon after the 1994 failure of the Clinton health care reform package.

A much smaller number of stories is initiated by journalists—more frequently print than television reporters—independently of the candidates. Stories about the budget deficit fit this category in 1988; stories about abortion, mainly used by reporters to gauge candidates' social conservatism, fit it in 1996. But except when voter expectations are dominant, the media policy priorities depicted in Table 5.2 (on page 84) reflect the topical emphases of candidates. As for candidates, it is clear that the electoral incentive drives their policy priorities. They discuss what voters demand when that demand is clear and unequivocal. Otherwise, they tend to evade important but politically risky issues, emphasizing instead those issues that their polls, focus groups, or best guesses, suggest will improve their election chances, as in 1988 and 1996. The 2000 election was unusual because the candidates engaged in a substantive debate on controversial issues despite a lack of voter demand. Peace and prosperity explain why candidates Bush and Gore faced no voter policy pressure. But the Bush campaign feared they could not defeat the incumbent's successor in good economic times without providing voters with a good reason to change parties. That is why they departed from the kind of policy evasion or miniaturization strategies typically seen when voter demand is low. The Bush team hoped to impress voters with bold proposals for a large tax cut, an ambitious missile defense system, and a Social Security privatization proposal. The intent was to demonstrate Bush's political courage and leaderly vision.[14]

ELECTORAL RATIFICATION

The second policy signal indicator involves evidence that candidate proposals relevant to voters' priorities are ratified by the election results, creating some measure of policy momentum. But as noted earlier, so many different

TABLE 5.3 VOTER AWARENESS OF TWENTY CANDIDATE ISSUE POSITIONS (1988, 1992, AND 1996 PRESIDENTIAL CAMPAIGNS)[1]

1988[2]	1992[3]	1996[4]
Capital punishment (B 78%)	Ban abortion (B 67%)	15% tax cut (Do 59%)
Midgetman missile (Du 63%)	Health insurance (C 66%)	Targeted tax cuts (C 55%)
No new taxes (B 60%)	50-cent gas tax (P 65%)	Mend don't end AA (C 54%)
Universal health care (Du 58%)	Tax the rich (C 65%)	Improve reading (C 54%)
No mandatory prayer (Du 53%)	Middle-class tax cut (C 60%)	More defense $ (Do 50%)
Good jobs/good wages (Du 53%)	Troops in Europe (B 59%)	Uniforms, curfews (C 48%)
Taxes last resort (Du 56%)	New world order (B 58%)	Abortion amend. (Do 48%)
Still in Cold War (B 46%)	5 yr. bal. budget (P 47%)	V-chip technology (C 46%)
Teacher fund (Du 41%)	College loans (C 46%)	Movie violence (Do 45%)
Line-item veto (B 39%)	Gains tax cut (B 45%)	Voters ok taxes (P 43%)
Collect more taxes (Du 49%)	Gays in military (C 45%)	Welfare tax break (C 41%)
Gun control (Du 49%)	100,000 new police (C 45%)	Ban illegals (Do 36%)
Soviet motives (Du 39%)	Parochial schools (B 41%)	New trade deals (P 36%)
Voluntary pledge (Du 38%)	Reduce budget deficit (B 38%)	Campaign reform (P 35%)
Flexible freeze (B 36%)	Cross-board cuts (B 33%)	Missile defense (Do 33%)
"100 days" program (Du 35%)	Econ. foreign policy (C 30%)	Intervention ok (C 32%)
30 million new jobs (B 30%)	Task forces (P 26%)	Cut entitlements (P 28%)
Conventional forces (Du 30%)	Stop racial politics (P 22%)	School choice $ (Do 25%)
Education president (B 29%)	Destroy missiles (P 13%)	Tax reform (P 24%)
Day-care tax credit (B 26%)	Rebuild Russia (P 9%)	Negative politics (P 18%)

[1]Twenty issue positions per year. % correct attributions to candidates by campaign's end in each election year in parentheses. B = Bush, C = Clinton, Do = Dole, Du = Dukakis, P = Perot.
[2]Source: Louis Harris Associates, 10/18/–11/4/1988; n = 1,875.
[3]Source: PSRA, 10/20–11/02/1992; n = 1,882.
[4]Source: PSRA, 10/21–11/02/1996; n = 1,881.

issues are discussed by candidates in campaigns—many of them unrelated to top voter priorities—that skeptics discount the possibility of clear mandates.[15] Table 5.3 illustrates the point by identifying no fewer than twenty of the most well-publicized candidate issue-positions for 1988, 1992, and 1996.

Isolating Mandates   Such ambiguity can be dispelled, however, by the right kind of data. An example would be evidence that there were one or more specific proposals with which the winning candidate had been clearly identified by a majority of potential voters prior to his election. Table 5.3 reports the percentages of survey respondents who correctly attributed issue positions to candidates in the days preceding each of the three presidential elections included in the Markle study. The table shows that seven, seven, and five issue positions were correctly attributed to winning candidates by pre-election majorities in the 1988, 1992, and 1996 elections, respectively. From this we might reasonably infer that most who voted for each year's winner knew before voting that he was identified with those particular issue positions, and were therefore potential if not proven endorsers of the positions.

The mandate claim is further strengthened if there is hard prevote evidence that a majority of voters personally endorsed the position as well as the candidate. Table 5.4 (on page 90) shows that in 1996, the only year that Markle collected such voter preference data, that Bill Clinton took just two issue stands that were both correctly attributed to him and majority-endorsed: a $2.75 billion spending plan to improve the reading skills of children in Kindergarten through third grade, and a "targeted tax cut" proposal for poor working families and middle-class families with children, as well as tax credits for college tuition, all to be financed with specific budget cuts.

Mandates Can Be Peripheral   The kind of information reported in Tables 5.3 and especially Table 5.4 enables us to pin down winners' mandates quite explicitly, something the 1996 survey was designed to do. But more importantly, it also shows that such mandates do not necessarily capture the most important policy action implications of an election. The reason has been noted throughout: candidates are issue-opportunists. They search out and emphasize the most popular stances and avoid discussing the most difficult problems, even those identified as priorities by voters, whenever they safely can. Many of the best known and most accurately attributed issue positions in Table 5.3—e.g., Bush's 1992 abortion stance, or Clinton's 1996 grade-school reading improvement proposal—were embraced and advertised by these candidates precisely because polls and focus groups showed them to be popular with target constituencies well before the candidates took the positions.

But voters' "favorite" candidate proposals, like those with which they happen to be most familiar, are not likely to address those problems the same voters identify as most in need of the next president's attention. Prompted by pollsters' questions that evoke reflection on the interests of the nation as a whole, voters are quite capable of thinking in terms of the public interest. But candidates know what Table 5.4 implies: that absent unusual circumstances, most voters think differently at the point of choosing among candidates. Many are more readily tempted by the promise of benefits that touch their lives. Further, the kind of problems atop the national priority list in recent years, such as reducing the deficit or improving the economy, often imply a need to allocate not benefits but sacrifices, such as tax increases or spending cuts.

Unless forced by unusual voter demand of the sort most recently evinced in 1992, then, candidates will avoid such proposals and feature positive inducements like the Clinton proposals just mentioned. Clinton's 1996 success with his "bite-sized" agenda of voter inducements led off-year (1997) and mid-term (1998) gubernatorial candidates in New Jersey, Virginia, and Texas to follow suit, emphasizing such promises as reduced automobile taxes, and avoiding proposals for addressing complex issues more central to

TABLE 5.4   PUBLIC SUPPORT FOR 1996 PRESIDENTIAL CANDIDATE ISSUE POSITIONS

ISSUE POSITION	PUBLIC SUPPORT FOR ISSUE POSITION	CORRECTLY ATTRIBUTED
Improve reading	71%	54% to Clinton
Welfare tax break	67	41 to Clinton
Targeted tax cuts	66	55 to Clinton
Voters ok taxes	65	43 to Perot
V-chip technology	62	46 to Clinton
Movie violence	61	45 to Dole
Negative politics	61	18 to Perot
Campaign reform	59	35 to Perot
Uniforms, curfews	58	48 to Clinton
Intervention ok	57	32 to Clinton
More defense $	55	50 to Dole
15% tax cut	51	59 to Dole
Ban illegals	51	36 to Dole
Tax reform	49	24 to Perot
Abortion amendment	49	48 to Dole
Mend don't end AA	48	54 to Clinton
Cut entitlements	48	28 to Perot
New trade deals	47	36 to Perot
School choice $	47	25 to Dole
Missile defense	35	33 to Dole

Source: PSRA, 10/21–11/02/1996; n = 1,881.

state priorities. Until 2000 Democratic candidate Bill Bradley criticized rival Democratic candidate and vice president Al Gore for lacking the kind of grand vision traditionally expected of presidents, Gore's list of issue positions was also tailored to addressing problems like traffic density and urban sprawl; problems, in other words, that are visible to voters in their daily lives.

All this shows why Table 5.2's measure of the extent of candidate participation in the priority problem consensus cannot be measured simply by the best known or most popular candidate proposals.

Inclusive Policy Signals   Data in Table 5.4 also introduce another piece of my argument: that we should not restrict the search for evidence of policy signals to the proposals of the election winner, or to proposals whose authorship is correctly identified by a majority of eligible voters. The table shows that substantial majorities personally endorse some candidate issue stands related to their own collective priorities (Table 5.2 on page 84) that were advocated by losers (e.g., the 65 percent endorsing Perot's idea that voters should approve changes in tax laws).

Majorities also endorse some proposals that are correctly attributed to candidates by far smaller percentages (e.g., 67 percent endorsed the idea of giving tax breaks to companies that hire people off the welfare rolls, but only 41 percent knew it was Clinton's proposal). Such findings imply that *elections can ratify policy directions independently of candidate or party fortunes*; that voters might well be disposed to support certain postelection actions regardless of who happens to win the election. Such was the situation in 1992, when losing candidate Perot did more than winner Clinton to set the postelection agenda for addressing Perot's signature issue, the budget deficit. Early in the campaign, Clinton had made it clear that he considered a 50-percent reduction in the deficit to be sufficient. He began toughening his antideficit rhetoric only after Perot managed to raise the issue's profile. The upshot was that, in effect, Clinton had a deficit reduction mandate forced upon him by the mass expectations that Perot helped to crystallize.[16]

The Perot case suggests that actionable policy signals could again emerge from a campaign and an election independently of who wins or who first makes the proposal.[17] That, to repeat, is why the "policy signal" concept transcends the idea of a winner's mandate. Finally, that is also why (to finish explaining an indicator introduced earlier) Table 5.2 measures the extent of candidate participation in the priority problem consensus by counting the total number of issue positions of *all* major candidates that are related in one way or another to voter priorities.

This same number can also be taken to indicate the extent to which the election ratifies a policy consensus, in that the more candidate rhetoric devoted to proposals that address the policy consensus, the greater the likelihood that action will be expected by the public and that the winner will feel pressure to address the consensus with action after the election. The more such proposals, in other words, the greater the likelihood that enough policy momentum will survive the election to be influential. Note that Table 5.2 shows there were about twice as many candidate proposals that converged with voter priorities in 1992 than in either other year. And in 1960, Kennedy and Nixon between them addressed a clear majority of their most important campaign proposals to the public's greatest concern: the Soviet threat. For that reason alone it was clear that whoever won, and by however small a margin (Kennedy won by one of the narrowest margins in history) the first priority would be to strengthen America's Cold War competitiveness.

POSTELECTION POLICY ACTION

Is it also the case that the more such voter-inspired proposals, the greater the likelihood of related postelection policy action? Postelection policy action is the third of the policy signal indicators, and Table 5.5 (on page 92) organizes information useful for assessing the action-value of prior consensus and electoral ratification. Four cases cannot settle the question. But the examples of 1960, 1988, 1992, and 1996 do suggest that when strong voter consensus elicits multiple related proposals, consistent policy action is indeed more likely.

For each year, the major piece of postelection legislative or other action most closely related to the top preelection voter priorities is identified. Also included are other significant legislative and nonlegislative policy initiatives intended to characterize (but not to exhaustively represent) the important policy action of the ensuing presidency.

Table 5.5 shows that 1960 and 1992 generated significantly more policy signals and other election-related policy action than did 1988 and 1996. Beginning with 1992, the need for deficit reduction had been discussed at length throughout the campaign, and the 1993 deficit reduction budget that observers and participants[18] later defined as a benchmark presidential achievement was the result. In fact, all of the most significant policy initiatives of the first Clinton administration—successful and unsuccessful—had been discussed in the campaign (see 1992 Clinton proposals in Table 5.3 on page 88). Similarly, 1960 generated a clear foreign policy signal, resulting in significant spending increases in military preparedness, nuclear capability and foreign and military assistance for allies and nations threatened by Soviet expansionism. Though not the result of majority public demand, Kennedy's 1963 civil rights proposal, which became law in 1964, was at least indirectly encouraged by the campaign events described earlier.

TABLE 5.5   POSTELECTION NATIONAL GOVERNMENT POLICY ACTION
(1960, 1988, 1992, AND 1996 PRESIDENTIAL ELECTIONS)

1988	1992
Cold war steward[1]	1993 deficit reduction budget[1]
Capital gains tax cut[3]	Welfare reform[1]
90 budget agreement[4]	Economic foreign policy[2]
Savings & Loan bailout[4]	Health care reform[3]
Clean Air Act[4]	
Gulf War[4]	
Flag burning amendment[5]	

1996	1960
Kosovo Action[2]	Increased defense spending[1]
Education spending[2]	Increased nuclear capability[1]
1997 balanced budget deal[4]	Increased foreign & military aid[1]
Entitlement reform[5]	1963 Civil Rights proposal[2]
	1963 tax cut proposal[4]

[1]Policy discussed in campaign adopted.
[2]Policy implied in campaign adopted.
[3]Policy discussed in campaign not adopted.
[4]Policy not discussed in campaign adopted.
[5]Policy not discussed in campaign introduced but not adopted.

The post-1988 Bush administration, on the other hand, drew little policy momentum from a campaign not forced to respond to public demand. Only Bush's frequently repeated campaign assertion that "the Cold War is not over" might be construed as advertising his foreign policy expertise and forecasting, in a general way, the careful stewardship that helped bring a peaceful conclusion to the Cold War. Bush did put forward—unsuccessfully—his campaign proposal for a capital gains tax cut. But the most significant policy actions of his presidency other than his Cold War stewardship—the 1990 budget agreement that came to be regarded as the first major step toward solving the deficit problem, the savings and loan bailout, and the Gulf War undertaken to drive Saddam Hussein from Kuwait—had no roots in the 1988 campaign. The story for 1996 is similar. Given that public priorities were less widely shared and less intensely held than in 1960 or 1992, and therefore generated fewer reactive candidate proposals, it was foreordained that the second Clinton administration would not be bringing any ratified policy signals to the proposal stage. The first major achievement of the second Clinton administration, the informal 1997 balanced budget agreement, was not an explicit topic of discussion in the 1996 campaign, although the case can be made that public support for Clinton's position in the budget fight with Congress in 1995 and early 1996, combined with the fact of his reelection, greatly strengthened his hand in negotiating the 1997 agreement. Entitlement reform, arguably the most pressing national priority at the time, received virtually no attention from the 1996 candidates, though some related proposals were publicly discussed but not voted on by Congress during the second Clinton term. Only issues that were not near the top of 1996 voters' highest priorities—policies implied by campaign rhetoric but not explicitly discussed—were later adopted. The U.S.-led 1999 bombing campaign to stop the Serbian assault on Albanians in Kosovo, for example, was consistent with Clinton's campaign assertion that intervention abroad is justified when American leadership can mean the difference between peace and war, and when it is consistent with American values and strategic interests. Similarly, some of the increased education spending Clinton wrung out of the Republican Congress in post-1996 budget negotiations (e.g., money for additional teachers for fiscal year 2000) were broadly consistent with education spending proposals made during the 1996 campaign (e.g., spending to improve the reading skills of children in Kindergarten through third grade).

The following proposition about postelection policy action is worth continued scrutiny: the greater the preelection consensus and the larger the number of associated candidate proposals, the greater the number of postelection initiatives (thus completing the policy signal) and, in addition, the greater the likelihood of successful policy initiatives that address top national priorities.

CONCLUSION

We see, then, that campaigns can generate policy momentum in ways that transcend the limits of traditional policy mandates. The models are 1960 and 1992, when anxious voters converged on top priorities—confirmed by polls and reinforced by media coverage—that candidates felt compelled to address with promises and proposals.

What matters is not which candidate proposes particular priorities or actions, or even who wins the election. Instead the driving force is the consensus forged by voter demand. Such demand is the surest guarantor of good campaigns. Except in rare circumstances like 2000, when one major candidate saw an advantage in proposing a bold policy agenda, a push from the electorate is likely to be a necessary condition for a serious policy debate.

That raises the last set of prior questions I must address before asking how to get voters to push for good campaigns ahead of every election. What kind of signals do voters have to send in order to get a serious policy response from the leading presidential candidates? If we assume that not all poll-tested public wishes are equally compelling, then how do candidates know when they may safely ignore, and when they must respond to expressions of public concern? What does it take to stop the hopefuls from pressing to shape public preferences and focus instead on responding to them? These questions concern us next.

NOTES

1. Elmer E. Schattschneider, *The Semisovereign People: A Realist's View of Democracy in America* (New York: Holt, Rinehart, and Winston, 1960).
2. Robert A. Dahl, "Myth of the Presidential Mandate," *Political Science Quarterly* 105 (1990), pp. 355–372.
3. Nelson W. Polsby and Aaron Wildavsky, *Presidential Elections*, 8th ed. (New York: Free Press, 1996).
4. David E. Rosenbaum, "Clinton Could Claim a Mandate, But It Might Be Hard to Define," *New York Times*, 1 November 1992, p. 18.
5. Patricia Heidotting Conley, *Presidential Mandates: How Elections Shape the National Agenda* (Chicago: University of Chicago Press, 2001).
6. Charles O. Jones, *The Presidency in a Separated System* (Washington, D.C.: Brookings, 1994), p. 181.
7. Richard M. Nixon, *Six Crises* (New York: Pyramid Books, 1962), pp. 315–461.
8. George H. Gallup, *Public Opinion 1935–1971*, vol. 3 (New York: Random House, 1972), p. 1671.
9. Bruce Buchanan, *Electing a President: The Markle Commission Research on Campaign '88* (Austin, TX: University of Texas Press, 1991), p. 90.
10. George C. Edwards, *Changing Their Minds: The Failure of the Bully Pulpit* (New Haven: Yale University Press, forthcoming).
11. Bruce Buchanan, *Electing a President: The Markle Commission Research on Campaign '88* (Austin, TX: University of Texas Press, 1991).
12. Center for Media and Public Affairs, "Report to the Markle Foundation" (Washington, D.C.: 1994).

13. Center for Media and Public Affairs, "Campaign '96: The Media and the Candidates. Final Report to the Markle Foundation" (Washington, D.C.: 1998).
14. Annenberg School for Communication, University of Pennsylvania, 2000 Presidential Campaign Debriefing, January 2001.
15. See, for example, Nelson W. Polsby and Aaron Wildavsky, *Presidential Elections*, 8th ed. (New York: Free Press, 1996), p. 315.
16. Bruce Buchanan, "A Tale of Two Campaigns," *Political Psychology* 16 (1995), pp. 297–319.
17. A related but not exactly equivalent phenomenon is more familiar: endorsement by winning candidates of issues initiated by third parties or rival candidates that faltered. In the 1996 Republican primaries, for example, Steve Forbes raised the profile of tax policy within the Republican Party to such an extent that party nominee Bob Dole later made a tax cut proposal the centerpiece of his campaign.
18. See, for example, Gerald F. Seib, "Clinton's Gamble: How It Shaped the '96 Race," *Wall Street Journal,* 30 October 1996, p. A-20; Robert E. Rubin, "The Clinton Growth Plan," *Wall Street Journal*, 31 October 1996, p. A-22.

6

VOTER LEVERAGE

THE CREDIBLE THREAT

Evidence is abundant that candidates and other political elites influence mass publics.[1] It has also been shown that certain features of media coverage—especially priming (the more prominent an issue is in the national information stream, the greater will be the weight accorded it in making political judgments) and framing (how the news defines or "frames" an issue significantly influences decisions people make about it)—affect audiences' policy priorities and political evaluations.[2]

Less often noticed, however, is the more widely scattered but equally impressive evidence of mass influence on elites; ranging from recent evidence of a general tendency for national policy to track public opinion[3] to historical episodes of "Constitutionally significant" mass mobilizations that reshaped American politics,[4] to contemporary strategic uses of public sentiment, as revealed by polls and focus groups, to fashion candidate messages.[5]

In the most fundamental sense, the state of voter expectations always shapes the nature of presidential campaigns. Candidates and news organizations strive, after all, to discern and tailor their presentations to fit the varying moods of the electorate. The cases we have examined show, however, that voter control of the policy agenda is not a given. When, as is often the case, the mass mood is relatively passive and disengaged, candidates search for issues and themes that can get attention and "move the numbers." Less often, voters *en masse* demand attention to particular policy problems, and both candidates and news organizations take respectful note. The reason, of course, is that American market and electoral systems make both politicians and journalists almost completely reliant on mass endorsement in one form or another to achieve their goals. Candidates must reach and influence voters to be elected. And to prosper, media must design campaign coverage with audience reaction in mind.

These facts make it possible, in theory at least, for voters to dictate the tone and content of candidate and media presentations. But that rarely happens.

Impotent Preferences

The reason is that not every expression of the public will commands the respect of politicians or news executives. Many, perhaps most, are inconclusive, akin to what one student of public opinion called "nonattitudes," conjured on the spot to answer pollsters' questions on subjects not previously given much thought. A good example is the typically fragmented pattern of responses to pollsters' questions about "the most important problems facing the country," a key indicator of the prospects for an election-year policy signal. The results of an October 1999 Pew Research Center survey showed 20 percent identifying "Social Security and Medicare" as the top priority, 15 percent "education," 13 percent "morality," 12 percent "the economy," 11 percent "health care," 9 percent "poverty," 7 percent "crime" and 6 percent "taxes."[6] Though some choosing each category were no doubt expressing heartfelt and well-considered opinions, it is very likely that many others were responding without great forethought, simply choosing the policy option that struck them as worthy at the moment. In any case, the message likely to be taken from such an incoherent list is that public opinion on policy priorities is not much of a constraint on the candidates, since ". . . no overarching issue emerges as the electorate's number one priority."[7]

Even majority opinion is often ignored by officials. For example, despite longstanding majority support for campaign finance reform, Congress remained deadlocked on the issue between the 1995 introduction of the McCain-Feingold measure until March 2002, when a reform bill won final Congressional approval and the promise of a presidential signature.[8] In the end, public support had far less to do with the success of reform than did other factors. One was the Enron scandal, which shined a timely spotlight on the unsavory link between campaign contributions and corporate political influence. Another was President Bush's announcement that he would sign the reform bill, thus discouraging otherwise certain Republican opposition in Congress. A third was the fact that prior to 2002, House members always passed the bill first and left it to the Senate to bail them out by killing the bill. But in 2002 the Senate passed the bill first, making it difficult for House members to vote no without looking like hypocrites for previously voting yes. Why was public support for campaign finance reform discounted? Because while the issue was stalemated in Congress, it had no obvious effect on the electoral fortunes of politicians who worked either for or against it.

Another example of discounted majority sentiment involves the not-uncommon expression by majorities of their willingness to abridge certain freedoms guaranteed by the Bill of Rights. In one recent poll, 70 percent of respondents said they would favor allowing courts to impose fines for "inaccurate or biased reporting."[9] No mainstream politician has proposed such action, which would entail limiting free speech, and there is little evidence that anyone has suffered political damage for failing to do so.

CREDIBLE THREATS

There are expressions of public sentiment, however, that do carry decisive weight with candidates and other political elites because they are taken as authoritative. Expectations like those associated with the Soviet threat and the economy in 1960 and 1992 are examples; these are expectations that candidates and public officials perceive as real demands, rather than as mere opinions. My proposition is that *politicians will feel compelled to take direction from public opinion if and only if they understand it to embody widespread, clear, and stable expectations that are backed by a credible threat of electoral consequences.*

Far from pandering to public opinion by tailoring their policy decisions to poll results, politicians, according to one recent and widely cited study, do just the opposite: They routinely ignore the public's policy preferences and follow their own political philosophies, as well as those of their party's activists, their contributors, and their interest group allies.[10] The authors of the study do concede that elections can exact a measure of responsiveness during the "brief intervals" that precede them. But the examples of 1988 and 1996 argue that even elections—which threaten loss of power, the ultimate political punishment—will not significantly increase elite respect for public opinion unless it embodies clear, stable, and widely shared expectations. Unless the evidence for such expectations is undeniable, and unless it is interpreted by politicians as a credible threat (as in the oft-described status of Social Security as the "third rail" of American politics—touch it and you die), they will refrain from concluding that the usually quiescent public is ready to exact the ultimate price. Consider the following examples of how and why public opinion gets dismissed as inconsequential.

CLEAR EXPECTATIONS

The American people are generally not impressed with the U.S. Congress's handling of the major problems and challenges that face the country.[11] Despite this adverse judgment, however, there is little evidence that members of Congress have tried to respond by changing their behavior, either individually or collectively. Why not?

One reason is that the disapproval has not been accompanied by clear demand that corrective steps be taken to improve the unsatisfactory performance. It is not enough merely to complain the Congress doesn't measure up, or that the campaign finance system is corrupt. Also required is evidence of strong public insistence that the authorities must actually take action. Without a perception that the people are calling for action, change remains unlikely.

STABLE EXPECTATIONS

Dissatisfaction with Congress has surely been a durable public sentiment.[12] If clear expectations for improvement had accompanied the dissatisfaction and achieved similar stability, Congress would have transformed itself by now. Fleeting public sentiment of any kind, on the other hand, is easily dismissed as inconsequential and is usually ignored. In one of the first widely publicized readings of public opinion on the subject, for example, a December 1999 *Wall Street Journal*–NBC News poll found that by a margin of 50 to 38 percent, Americans thought Congress should approve the U.S.–China trade deal.[13] But in order for that particular "clear expectation" to become a significant factor in the then-pending Congressional debate on the issue, it would first have to achieve stability; that is, it would have to prove its staying power in the face of efforts by contending interests to change it. As it happened, opinion held firm and the China trade arrangement was passed. But mass opinion played little role in securing passage, both because the president had the votes without the need to evoke public pressure, and because majority Congressional opinion had congealed even before public sentiment was measured.

Just to get the attention of policymakers, public sentiment must be as clear and as repetitive as commercial advertising. To force them to recognize that action is expected, that expectation must be just as durable and unmistakable as the evidence of public unhappiness with the problem. But for all of that, the peoples' representatives are still not likely to act unless the probable costs of inaction are obvious and painful enough to be unacceptable.

ELECTORAL CARROTS AND STICKS

If members of Congress believed that failure to meet clear expectations for changes in their institution would result in loss of their seats, most would quickly do what was necessary to keep their seats. But since "[i]ndividual members [keep winning] re-election year after year" no matter what,[14] there are no meaningful consequences associated with failure to change, and thus no incentives to change.

Consequences involve both carrots (attaining or winning power) and sticks (losing or failing to attain power). But it is the stick—the fear of losing or not achieving the carrot—that most surely encourages responsiveness to public expectations.

Public opinion that signals a credible threat can even move that branch of government most effectively designed to resist it—the judicial branch. It is only necessary that the opinion in question be taken to imply a possibility of public action that Court members interpret as threatening to the Court's legitimacy or power.

The expression of public opinion that best illustrates this point was that which produced Franklin D. Roosevelt's landslide reelection in 1936. Emboldened by the overwhelming public affirmation of the very New Deal policies that had consistently been declared unconstitutional by the conservative Supreme Court majority in place at the time, FDR proposed legislation to "pack" the Court with additional, younger justices more likely to be sympathetic to his policy designs. The court-packing plan was widely condemned and eventually failed. But at least one justice—Owen Roberts—apparently found the vote-inspired threat to the Court's autonomy credible enough to provoke a change of heart. His switch in one pivotal case was the first step toward a shift in the Court's balance of power. Soon thereafter, the Court was consistently upholding Roosevelt's reforms.[15]

Clarity, stability, and threat are difficult conditions for public opinion to achieve with any regularity, given its typically fragmented, vague, disorganized, and ephemeral nature.[16] Nevertheless, they do come together from time to time. All three conditions were approximated, for example, during the 1992 presidential campaign. Recall reporter Robin Toner's summary judgment: "From the New Hampshire primary on [stability], the voters provided a merciless reality check on the candidates; those who strayed from the economy [clear expectation] for very long were quickly punished [consequences]."[17] The conditions were also implicit in the climate of opinion during the 1960 campaign. The public desire that the government deal more effectively with the Soviet challenge had been clear to elites since the 1957 launching of *Sputnik* (stability). And the fear that he might lose the election (threat) because of the perception that Eisenhower had not met the challenge prompted Nixon to devote a substantial portion of his campaign to proposing policies intended to convince the voters that he, not Kennedy, was best equipped to face down the Russians.

NONCAMPAIGN CASES

Let us consider two additional cases, both from outside the immediate campaign context that will further clarify and elaborate the conditions under which public opinion does and does not push elected leaders into the reactive mode.

THE 1997 BUDGET AGREEMENT

The backdrop for the budget agreement of 1997 was the confrontation between President Clinton, a Democrat, and the Republican Congress that shut down the government twice; once in late 1995, and again in early 1996. Although budget battles are typically waged in the language of revenues and expenditures, the real argument between Clinton and the Republican Congress that came to power in 1994 concerned the proper role of government in society. To Clinton, government was a positive force. Taxes were not too high; indeed they were vital to finance public goods such as education and social services. To congressional Republicans, government is an impediment to social and economic advancement. Taxes and bureaucracy should be shrunk, leaving people to decide for themselves how to spend their earnings. That, as they see it, is the best way to unleash market forces that benefit all.

How could such a fundamental philosophical disagreement, which had paralyzed the budget process and poisoned the political atmosphere since the early years of the Reagan administration, suddenly find itself at least temporarily resolved within the framework of a bipartisan agreement to balance the budget by the year 2002?

The first hint of change was an unexpected drop in the budget deficit, a drop caused by unforeseen tax revenues from a booming economy, with larger-than-expected revenues suddenly projected to continue through the year 2002 and beyond. That meant that previously unthinkable agreements were no longer beyond the realm of possibility. Clinton, for example, could afford to accept Republican cuts in capital gains taxes and estate taxes. And Republicans could bring themselves to swallow additional billions for such measures as expanding health care for low-income children, and $1,500 tax credits for each of the first two years of college tuition. In brief, windfall tax revenues meant that each side could now allow the other to have much of what it wanted without surrendering its own priorities. What is more, there was enough of a revenue stream left over to project a zero deficit by 2002.

There were intense partisans on both sides who saw any agreement as ideological treason despite the revenue windfall. These people wanted to keep fighting. But in the end, the leaders decided not only to deal, but also to label the result a "bipartisan" agreement. Why? *Because they feared a public backlash against continued partisan bickering and stalemate.* Neither side was eager to risk the public wrath that would probably follow another government shutdown. Both had learned to regard poll evidence of public displeasure with the prospect of additional government shut-downs with special respect—indeed as too dangerous to ignore. The reason was that *both sides perceived that the public had made the Republicans pay a price at the polls for the government shutdowns of 1995 and 1996.* The pain of electoral defeat in 1996 had made the threat of similar future punishment entirely credible to the negotiators, and it shaped their deliberations, facilitating an agreement. They sought a public relations benefit from projecting an image of bipartisan harmony. That, they hoped, would appeal to a mass public thoroughly fed up with partisan bickering.

Interestingly, the same negotiators were not at all intimidated by another poll-tested expression of the public will they considered far less threatening: opposition to tax cuts. The fact that spring 1997 public opinion polls showed most voters not strongly supportive of tax cuts was not enough to lead either President Clinton or the Congressional Republicans to abandon the tax cut plans that were key parts of the agreement. Both sides were quite willing to risk public disapproval by endorsing big tax cuts in 1997 for the same reason that such 2000 Republican presidential candidates as George W. Bush and Steve Forbes put forward tax cut proposals despite continuing poll evidence of public attitudes ranging from disinterest to disapproval. When it came to tax cuts, there was no fear of public retaliation because the voters' messages were mixed. Conventional wisdom certainly did not regard 1996 Republican candidate Bob Dole's 15 percent across-the-board income tax cut proposal as figuring in his defeat at the polls. Indeed, Table 5.4 (on page 90) shows that in the days just before the 1996 election, a narrow majority—51 percent—expressed support for Dole's proposal. By 2000, tax cut support had dwindled. Most national polling in the run-up to the 2000 election showed tax policy to be a low public priority, and uncovered little public passion for or against the idea of tax cuts. That left candidates like George W. Bush and Steve Forbes free to use tax cut proposals to appeal to partisan enthusiasts during the Republican primaries. And it allowed eventual nominee Bush to feature his tax cut as an enticement to economic conservatives secure in the knowledge that there would be no politically costly public backlash.

THE 1998 IMPEACHMENT DECISION

Many Republicans, eager to impeach President Clinton for perjury and obstruction of justice in the Monica Lewinsky affair, sought evidence of public support for that move in the results of the midterm elections of 1998. When their party unexpectedly lost a net total of five seats to Democrats, Republican Party leaders in and outside Congress saw it as clear evidence that the public did not want the president removed from office. Opinion polls also showed strong majority opposition to impeachment or resignation, *prima facie* evidence that the public did not want the president ousted. Shortly after the elections, a number of moderate Republican Congressmen signaled that they would not vote for impeachment articles if they came to a vote in the House of Representatives. Few admitted it plainly, but the subtext was fear of eventual retribution at the polls. As columnist William Safire concluded, "Most will base their vote against impeachment less on the rule of law than on a simple judgment: whether this helps or hurts them in the next election."[18]

Later, conservative party leaders increased the pressure on the moderates to support impeachment. Shortly thereafter the House Judiciary Committee voted out impeachment articles, and moderates began to reverse course, with most eventually voting to support impeachment. What explains their change of heart? The reasons varied from one representative to the next. They included irritation at Clinton's continuing refusal to admit that he had perjured himself, the fear of losing party support needed for reelection or other career advancement, a growing sense among some that Constitutional duty required it and the common belief that conviction of the president in the Senate remained unlikely due to continued public opposition.

Perhaps most telling, however, was an argument slowly gaining currency among Republicans that their initial fear of certain electoral reprisal was probably not justified.

For those in "safe" districts, the biggest political threat was from within their own party, in the primary elections.[19] A great many Republican Congressmen were from districts where a vote to impeach would be popular. And reassuring to those from competitive districts that had supported President Clinton in 1996 was the view that any political fallout from the inquiry would diminish to insignificance long before the next national election. Public opposition to impeachment, though remarkably stable and widespread, had not shown the kind of passion or intensity needed to keep it in play long enough to influence an election then nearly two years away. People were simply not invested enough in the outcome. Said one prominent Republican, "The attention span of Americans is 'Which movie is coming out next month?' and whether the quarterly report on their stock will change." In all probability, two years would be enough time for voters to be distracted by a succession of newly compelling concerns, including the fight to redefine the Republican Party and to capture its presidential nomination. Said a Republican campaign strategist in touch with House Republicans, "When we have a front-runner and a standard-bearer, the party will be cast in that person's image, not in the Judiciary Committee's image."[20] The emergence of Texas governor George W. Bush as the frontrunner after a spirited battle with Arizona Senator John McCain in the early primaries made that conclusion seem prophetic. But however the 2000 election turned out, the conclusion of relevance here would stand: When public opinion came to seem less threatening to their future electoral prospects, Congressional Republicans felt increasingly free to disregard it.

IMPLICATIONS

The budget and impeachment examples show the power of a threat of electoral reprisal for failure to meet specific expectations. They also show how closely that power is linked to the credibility of the threat. Credibility was present in the budget case because a price had recently been paid at the polls, making it seem very likely that a similar price would be exacted again unless the partisans reached an agreement. Credibility in the impeachment case, on the other hand, began to wane once the extended time lag between a vote to impeach and the opportunity for reprisal made punishment seem less likely.

CREDIBLE CAMPAIGN THREATS

Elections immediately follow campaigns, thus avoiding the sort of credibility erosion evident in the impeachment case. Elections also afford the opportunity to make the link between candidate performance and voter reward or punishment completely unambiguous. The threat of unsustainable vote loss can be made to appear direct and immediate. The risk of losing even a modest share of votes will seem significant to most candidates in most presidential races. As the 2000 presidential election reminds, the margin of victory can be razor-thin. This means that proportionately small numbers of voters can sometimes pose threats real enough to commandeer candidates. We saw that candidate Bill Clinton felt threatened enough to camouflage his campaign advertising in both 1992 and 1996 both to evade media attention and to avoid stirring the wrath of centrist independent voters fed up with negative ads. And both Bush and Gore thought it prudent in 2000 to tailor their prescription drug programs to Florida retirees who figured to hold the balance of power in that state before the postelection "train wreck" that muddied the waters, sending the Florida results, and the election, to the U.S. Supreme Court.

A closely divided electorate means that presidential candidates cannot afford to ignore even "niche" voter demands. While the electorate is evenly split, credible threats supportive of high-quality campaigns can be as influential as any pro-choice or right-to-life lobby. But candidates face complex trade-offs.

CANDIDATE CALCULATIONS

The likelihood of any candidate responding to a threat from any bloc of voters depends on that candidate's belief that responding will not alienate an equal or larger number of voters who disagree. This is especially clear in the case of specific policy stances on controversial measures like abortion. In 2000, Republican hopeful George W. Bush did not respond to minority-backed, right-to-life pressure to toughen his antiabortion stance because he believed that to do so would alienate more votes than it attracted (he was probably right). Reform-inspired pressure (for example, to get a candidate to swear off attack advertising) would evoke similar cost-benefit calculations. In general, the more widespread the pressure and the less controversial the desired response, the more likely is the candidate to respond.

CONSTRAINTS

Credible threats to electoral success posed by voters are the single most powerful source of leverage on the campaign behavior of any candidate. Recall the Chapter 4 discussion of Friedrich's[21] "principle of anticipated reactions." Candidates know that they must take the reactions they anticipate from voters into account before taking stands or taking action. But again, *citizen demand is only infrequently clear, stable, and threatening enough at any level of consensus to make it plain to candidates that they must respond in specific ways to avoid unacceptable costs.* When prospective voters are moved in large numbers to pose and evince the will to enforce such threats, as in 1960 or 1992, candidates are sure to respond. But the comparatively passionless and inchoate state of citizen opinion evident during the presidential campaigns of 1988, 1996, and 2000 is much more typical.

Because voters usually aren't moved even to specify, let alone to enforce their preferences, candidates are left with considerable discretion. Out of this discretion has evolved a style of campaigning that features heavy doses of manipulation, deception, attack advertising, issue evasion and demagoguery.[22] People consistently say they do not like this brand of politics. "Our polls showed that one of the things that was driving down interest and essentially keeping people out of the process was this sense of 'I just don't like what's been happening in politics, I just don't like it,'" said political scientist Thomas E. Patterson, co-director of an election-year 2000 investigation of public reactions to the presidential campaign.[23]

Not all candidates are fairly described as unscrupulous. An ambitious survey of more than 20,000 recent candidates for public office at all but the presidential level, including both winners and losers and representatives of all political parties, uncovered a notable degree of ethical sensitivity in candidate descriptions of their own standards of acceptable campaign practice. The researchers also present case studies that illustrate the tough strategic and ethical choices many campaigns are forced to make, and the extraordinary pressures created by the struggle for victory.[24]

The fact is, however, that such pressures often lead candidates at every level to disregard clear voter preferences in campaign style. They do so because winning requires it, and because they can get away with it. As we saw in the case of unhappiness with Congress, mere voter likes and dislikes, in the absence of clear expectations for corrective action "or else," do not command the respect of politicians. They are nothing more than impotent preferences.

CONCLUSION

Voters bring the weakest incentives and the sketchiest preparation to the work of the electoral triangle. Yet representative democracy gives them the lion's share of responsibility. They are expected to select and supervise qualified leaders. They are expected to help ensure that public policy serves the national interest. Because access to the presidency requires their votes, they have the formal power to meet these expectations. But the point of this chapter has been that real democratic control can result only when voter demands on elites take the strict form—clarity, durability, and the threat of punishment—detailed earlier.

Our political traditions have neither encouraged nor equipped American voters to deliberately and self-consciously initiate and coordinate such disciplined signals on their own. The credible threats that have been signaled by voters to candidates in the past have seldom if ever resulted from conscious intent or strategic calculation. They emerged spontaneously out of mass responses to events and circumstances when they emerged at all. The idea that voters, who the influential democratic theorist Joseph Schumpeter once dismissed as "incapable of anything other than a stampede," could self-consciously muster such collective political will on a regular basis is widely thought to be naive. They may have the power, but they lack the unity of will and the coordinative capability for collective action on such a scale.

But despite this pervasive skepticism and doubt, it is indeed possible, at least in principle, to better and more consistently engage citizens as both voters and shapers of important policy. There are, to be sure, significant obstacles to such a project. Moreover, there are no magic bullets or quick fixes. Still, as I show next in conclusion, the capability exists.

NOTES

1. See, for example, John R. Zaller, *The Nature and Origins of Mass Opinion* (New York: Cambridge, 1992); Richard A. Brody, *Assessing the President* (Stanford, CA: Stanford University Press, 1991).
2. Joseph N. Cappella and Kathleen Hall Jamieson, *Spiral of Cynicism: The Press and the Public Good* (New York: Oxford, 1997); Shanto Iyengar, *Is Anyone Responsible?* (Chicago, IL: University of Chicago Press, 1991); Shanto Iyengar and Donald Kinder, *News That Matters* (Chicago: University of Chicago Press, 1987).
3. Benjamin I. Page and Robert Y. Shapiro, *The Rational Public* (Chicago, IL: University of Chicago Press, 1992).
4. Cf., Bruce Ackerman, *We the People* (Cambridge, MA: Harvard University Press, 1991); Walter Dean Burnham, "Pattern Recognition and 'Doing' Political History: Art, Science, or Bootless Enterprise?" in *The Dynamics of American Politics*, ed. Lawrence C. Dodd and Calvin Jillson (Boulder, CO: Westview Press, 1994).
5. See, for example, Dick Morris, *Behind the Oval Office* (New York: Random House, 1997).
6. Pew Research Center for the People and the Press, "Retropolitics: The Political Typology: Version 3.0" (Washington, D.C., 1999), p. 130.
7. Ibid., p. 5.
8. Alison Mitchell, "Campaign Finance Bill Wins Final Approval in Congress and Bush Says He'll Sign It," *New York Times*, 21 March 2002, p. A-1.
9. Media Monitor, "What Do People Want from the Press?" (Washington, D.C.: Center for Media and Public Affairs, May/June 1997).
10. Lawrence R. Jacobs and Robert Y. Shapiro, *Politicians Don't Pander* (Chicago, IL: University of Chicago Press, 2000), p. 296.
11. Morris P. Fiorina and Paul E. Peterson, *The New American Democracy* (Boston: Allyn and Bacon, 1998), p. 410.
12. Glen Parker and Roger Davidson, "Why Do Americans Love Their Congressman so Much More Than Their Congress?" *Legislative Studies Quarterly* 4 (1979), pp. 52–61.
13. Ronald G. Shafer, "Washington Wire: The Wall Street Journal–NBC News Poll," *Wall Street Journal*, 17 December 1999, p. A-1.
14. David Broder, "Public Opinion's Role," *Austin American-Statesman*, 15 December 1998, p. A-15.
15. Rayman L. Solomon, "Court-Packing Plan," in *The Oxford Companion to the Supreme Court*, ed. Kermit L. Hall (New York: Oxford University Press, 1992), p. 203.
16. John R. Zaller, *The Nature and Origins of Mass Opinion* (New York: Cambridge, 1992).
17. Robin Toner, "Political Metamorphoses: Voters Impose Discipline on the Candidates as Perot Finds a New Way of Campaigning," *New York Times*, 3 November 1992, p. A1.
18. William Safire, "King of Chutzpah," *New York Times*, 30 November 1998, p. A-27.

19. Jackie Calmes, "House Divided: Why Congress Hews to the Party Lines on Impeachment," *Wall Street Journal*, 16 December 1998, p. A-1.
20. Richard L. Berke, "Many in G.O.P. See No Fallout for 2000 Vote," *New York Times*, 14 December 1998, p. A-1.
21. Carl Friedrich, *Constitutional Government and Democracy*, 2nd ed. (Boston: Ginn, 1941).
22. For an extended analysis of hard-edged presidential campaign practices and their costs to the political system, see Bruce Buchanan, *Renewing Presidential Politics: Campaigns, Media, and the Public Interest* (Lanham, MD: Rowman and Littlefield, 1996), pp. 91–114.
23. Robin Toner, "Just How Well Did the System Work?" *New York Times*, 12 March 2000, p. 30.
24. Ronald A. Faucheux and Paul S. Herrnson, eds., *Campaign Battle Lines: The Practical Consequences of Crossing the Line between What's Right and What's Not in Political Campaigning* (Washington, D.C.: Campaigns & Elections, 2002); Ronald A. Faucheux and Paul S. Herrnson, eds., *The Good Fight: How Political Candidates Struggle to Win Elections without Losing Their Souls* (Washington, D.C.: Campaigns & Elections, 2002).

CIVIC DUTY

A Strategy for Change

Electoral reform is an American tradition. It has always been sought in the name of democracy, and it has usually focused on empowering citizens. Three of the most durable reform goals, for example, have been to increase access to voting and voter turnout, to strengthen mass relative to elite influence on the selection of candidates, and to make election campaigns more informative and policy-relevant, so that voters might better grasp the policy implications of their electoral choices.

The best examples of the first are the several expansions of the franchise by Constitutional amendment, which made previously excluded groups eligible to vote. They include the Fifteenth Amendment forbidding states to deny voting rights based on race (1870), the Nineteenth Amendment giving women the right to vote (1920), and the Twenty-sixth Amendment lowering the voting age to eighteen (1971). Other examples are voting reforms like the elimination of state poll tax laws, and the 1993 National Voter Registration Act (known as the "Motor-Voter" law), which were intended to increase the incidence of registration and voting by reducing the barriers to each.

Most notable among the recent reforms seeking to shift the balance of power from elites to citizens was the post-1968 adoption by the major political parties of rules that require the nomination of presidential candidates selected by voters in primary elections rather than by party leaders in brokered conventions. But most often emphasized by media and politicians is campaign finance reform. Between 1995 and 2002, an intense effort was mounted to improve upon the Federal Elections Campaign Acts of 1971 and 1974, both Watergate-era campaign finance reform laws that were intended to keep citizen influence over elected officials from being diluted relative to the influence wielded by well-financed special interests. With the passage of the 2002 reform act, that effort finally succeeded. But many critics and some supporters expect that the issue has not been fully resolved, and legislation has been introduced in Congress to require broadcast organizations to provide some free television time to candidates, in hopes of further reducing the dominance of money in politics.

Twentieth-century innovations relevant to the third, "policy relevance" aim include the public interest provisions of the Radio Act of 1927 and its successor, the Communications Act of 1934, the virtual institutionalization of presidential candidate debates since 1976, and the voluntary free television time experiment orchestrated in 1996 by the Free TV for Straight Talk Coalition, which hoped to pressure candidates into more extensive discussion of policy problems and proposals. The idea that elections involve policy as well as candidate choices has roots in the emergence of the party system in the early Republic. The related twentieth-century reform efforts all stem from the realization that media and candidates tended to avoid potentially unprofitable or politically risky topics or forums unless prodded.

INDIFFERENT RESULTS

The results of these innovations and reforms have been disappointing, both to their sponsors and their critics. The many expansions of the franchise to previously excluded groups, for example, like simplified voter registration requirements, have yet to produce sustained increases in comparatively low U.S. voter turnout. To be sure, it is likely that voter turnout would be even lower, and participation even less demographically representative than it is, without such reforms as the several expansions of the franchise and the removal of poll tax barriers. The disappointment stems from international comparisons, which places the United States near the bottom.[1] Curtis Gans of the Committee for the Study of the American Electorate describes declining turnout as a "serious societal problem." He also notes that U.S. average turnout ranks 139th out of 167 democracies of any kind.[2]

The campaign finance reform laws of the 1970s, which imposed contribution limits and provided for full disclosure of all campaign receipts and expenditures, have been equally disappointing. They were diluted by the Supreme Court decision in *Buckley v. Valeo*, which declared unconstitutional any absolute limits on the freedom of individuals to spend their own money on campaigns, while setting a $1,000 limit on contributions by others to candidates. Another Supreme Court Decision, *Colorado Republican Party v. Federal Election Commission*, opened the floodgates of so called "soft money," which is money not subject to legal limitation or reporting requirements as long as the funds are not formally coordinated with a candidate's campaign. As a result, polls show that, despite the campaign finance law, as many as 75 percent of respondents still believe that "many public officials make or change policy decisions as a result of money they receive from major contributors."[3] It remains to be seen whether the 2002 reform legislation, which prohibits national political parties from accepting or spending any soft money, will truly staunch the flow of special interest funds to candidates. Some critics predicted that big donors would simply give money to less-accountable outside interest groups who face less-stringent disclosure requirements. It was also clear that the legislation would face court challenges from opponents.[4] As the November 6, 2002 implementation date of the new law approached, headlines predicted what proponents were sure to find a disappointing result: "Parties Create Ways to Avoid Soft Money Ban; State Groups to Collect Unlimited Donations."[5]

Satisfaction with the results of reforms and innovations on the policy information front have not been markedly greater. Only presidential candidate debates have produced impressively positive consequences by establishing themselves as the most compelling, and in some ways the most usefully informative, of all campaign spectacles. Debates inform by providing voters rare opportunities to watch candidates perform in less-scripted and controlled environments than speeches or advertisements. Debates can prompt candidates to respond extemporaneously, and to "think on their feet." The national television audience has been known to rely on debate performances to resolve doubts about particular candidates facing more experienced opponents, such as John F. Kennedy in 1960, and George W. Bush in 2002. Though policy issues are rarely probed in great detail, debate viewers with little prior exposure to candidate platforms can learn about issues as well.

The 1996 free television time experiment, a policy-centered innovation, brought some increase in candidate on-air attention to substantive issues. Content analysis showed, for example, that the candidates were three times as substantive, as well as twice as positive, as campaign coverage on the network evening newscasts.[6] But the candidates were still free to press the same self-interested policy themes and agendas they expounded in traditional formats. The resultant broadcasts were considered inconsequential by some candidates and prominent TV journalists. Most importantly, they were little-watched by the public.[7] Finally, "public interest" broadcast requirements have yet to result in campaign, election, or other public interest television coverage of the scope or quality that fair-minded critics deem sufficient to meet the information needs of an informed electorate.[8]

NEGLECT OF INCENTIVES

Why does electoral reform have such an indifferent record? The most important reason, as I suggested in the Preface, is that so few reforms effectively address the incentives of the major actors. For example, the ambiguity of campaign finance laws, together with the lack of meaningful penalties for noncompliance, often give candidates more reason to evade than to comply with them. The December 1998 decision of the Federal Election Commission not to require either major 1996 presidential campaign to repay multimillion-dollar, soft-money sums thought by commission auditors and the commission general counsel to be in excess of Federal campaign spending limits and to represent illegal coordination of their advertising with the two political parties illustrates well the continuing absence of compliance incentives.[9]

Similarly, enforcement of "public interest" broadcast requirements has been too inconsistent and too lenient to motivate a significant increase in the incidence or quality of public interest programming, especially during political campaigns. At various times, broadcasters have been required, by shifting regulations and guidelines derived from the act, to offer news and public affairs programs, to air educational programs for children, to devote time to controversial issues of public importance, to provide audiences with opportunities to hear responsible advocates on all sides of such issues, and to give equal time to all legally qualified candidates for a given office. The upshot is that the government's conception of what kind of broadcast content serves the public interest remains imprecise and controversial.[10] Left to their own devices, the news media continue to downplay policy. "The news media are offering the American public a fine education in campaign tactics," noted a report on a content study of early Campaign 2000 coverage by the Project for Excellence in Journalism, "but [are] telling them little about matters that actually will affect them as citizens . . . The press has provided only scant reporting on the candidates' backgrounds, records or ideas." Eighty percent of stories "focused on changes in tactics, who has more money or internal organizational problems," while only 13 percent offered information relevant to understanding the probable policy consequences of a given candidate's election.[11]

The incentives of citizens have received even less attention. The 1993 "Motor-Voter" law, for example, reduced the registration barrier significantly, making it easy for the 3.4 million previously unregistered citizens who acted before the 1996 election to sign up to vote as they conducted other business that brought them to government agencies.[12] But turnout went down, not up, in 1996, and increased only marginally in 2002, suggesting that the act itself has done little to make voting more attractive. "Its impact so far has been minimal," opined Curtis Gans of the Committee for the Study of the American Electorate, "because the real barriers to higher turnout are motivational, not structural."[13]

Similarly, the "Free Time for Straight Talk" effort made more information available, but did not increase the incentives of citizens to acquire it. Thus, only about 22 percent of registered voters reported watching one or more of the twenty-five free airtime appearances each made by Bill Clinton and Bob Dole throughout the 1996 general election campaign on CBS, NBC, CNN, PBS, and Fox (ABC did not offer free airtime to the candidates).[14]

Although there will always be large public questions worthy of discussion, the timetables of campaigns and elections do not always correspond to the natural ripening and deciding of the kind of major public policy questions that capture mass attention. Unless voters were to become conditioned to regard campaign seasons as *ipso facto* the right time for major policy debates, public use of an innovation like free TV time is likely to vary with voters' feelings of a "need to know."

RETHINKING REFORM

So, the reforms attempted to date have achieved indifferent results because they have not significantly altered the incentives of candidates, media, or voters. There is a good reason why they have not done so. It is that changing incentives requires serious disruption of the *status quo*. Most who have made serious attempts to bring about reform have felt the need to be realistic, which meant avoiding proposals too easily dismissed as utopian and impractical. The problem with such realism in the present context is that there are just two ways to bring about real changes in incentives, and neither can easily pass the "political feasibility" test. The first, government regulation of campaign behavior, is the most straightforward and potentially the most powerful. *Simply pass and vigorously enforce laws that require the desired behavior and make illegal all disapproved behavior.* This option is, of course, rejected out of hand because it would require constitutionally impermissible assaults on the First Amendment freedoms of the actors. By American law and custom, candidates cannot be forced to discuss issues or forbidden to attack opponents. Media cannot be instructed to cover issues or to avoid playing up strategy and conflict. And citizens cannot be required either to learn or to vote. Even the effort to regulate soft money passed in 2002 may not survive a First Amendment court test. It is worth noting, however, that such protections, however constitutionally unassailable here, do foreclose a powerful method of political quality control used in other democracies, such as banning certain forms of advertising, for example, and requiring citizens to vote.

The second option, the one I recommend and detail later in this chapter, is to devise a way to harness the only force other than government regulation that is powerful enough to alter the incentives of candidates and media: *citizen leverage.* Citizens have leverage, recall, because they ultimately control what the other actors want: votes and market share. This approach faces no constitutional or legal barriers; thus it can in principle be successfully advocated and implemented. The task is made easier by the fact that my proposal incorporates several existing reform initiatives, some of which are already widely supported. But in the end, candidate and media incentives cannot be altered without major changes in the political behavior of citizen-voters;

changes sure to be both controversial and difficult to achieve. Nevertheless, there is good reason to close this book with a detailed strategy for change. It is *to show what it would actually take* to reconfigure the electoral incentive system. A clear-eyed appreciation of the size of that task is required before deciding between reform and inaction. Bear in mind, however, that neither option is cost-free. If the cost of reform is a long-term struggle for uncertain success, the price of inaction is perpetuation of the *status quo*.

PLAN OF ATTACK

In the following sections I detail a three-step program intended to bring American democracy's incentive system more closely in line with its ideals. The goal, as stated in the Preface, is to *equip voters to use credible threats to evoke both real public policy debates and civil campaign practices in noncrisis as well as crisis circumstances.*

STEP ONE: REMOVE BARRIERS TO LEARNING AND VOTING

Increased voter learning is necessary not only because the effort helps to bind voters to the process, as argued in Chapter 4, but also because informed voters are better able to recognize the subtle as well as the obvious national problems worthy of their attention. Informed voters are also better equipped to demand more nuanced attention to policy from both media and candidates. And they are better positioned to recognize and discourage both candidate evasion and deception.

Increased voter turnout is important both because it helps expand regime support, and because high turnout better ratifies policy. The higher the turnout, the greater the legitimacy of any policy signals or mandates an election manages to produce.

Currently, half of the eligible electorate neither absorbs much campaign-related information nor votes in presidential elections. The first step, therefore, is to address the most significant citizen disincentives to learning and voting. *Institutional barriers* and *repellent candidate behavior* head the list.

Institutional Barriers   Of all the disincentives to learning and voting, institutional barriers are the most clearly understood and are well-addressed by measures already in place or recommended. Reforms like the "Motor-Voter" law do not themselves address incentives but they do clear obstacles that make it harder for other initiatives to do so. A related barrier-reduction step worth taking is to adopt the kind of fully automatic registration system already functioning successfully in many parts of the world.

Two other relevant innovations are vote-by-mail systems (already in place in six U.S. states) and early (i.e., pre-Election-Day) in-person voting, now allowed in seven states. Finally, many countries make Election Day an official holiday, and a Pew Charitable Trusts Task Force on Campaign Reform recently proposed that the United States follow suit, both because it would make voting easier and because the symbolic recognition might add to its attractiveness.[15]

Repellent Candidate Behaviors   While the growing scholarly evidence concerning the effectiveness of attack or negative advertising remains ambiguous,[16] most political practitioners still share the view expressed by Democratic opposition-research consultant Dan Carol: "A good, hard negative campaign about someone's record, burned in effectively, still works."[17] A study of Campaign 2000 political advertising by the Annenberg Public Policy Center said that 40.3 percent of the messages put up through March 2000 were attack ads, a higher percentage than at the same point in 1998.[18] Attacks are therefore still pervasive, despite the fact noted in Chapter 4 that most voters claim not to like them, and despite the likelihood that aggressive, hostile presentations discourage attention, interest, learning, and possibly also some voting, particularly among independents.[19]

Attacks can also discourage bold policy proposals. For example, former New Jersey Senator Bill Bradley, a candidate for the 2000 Democratic presidential nomination, released a detailed health care plan he hoped would position him to claim a mandate if he won, helping to soften opposition in Congress. The proposal immediately became a target for his nomination opponent, Vice President Al Gore, who spent months picking it apart. In the weeks before the first caucuses and primaries, Gore's attacks had "managed to muddle Mr. Bradley's message and knock him off stride."[20] Bradley was later judged to have lost the nomination fight in part because of that ambitious policy proposal. Future candidates are likely to take note.

Other candidate tactics voters dislike include deception, in all its various forms (e.g., misrepresentation, half-truths, outright lying), which is as pervasive as attacks.[21] Jamieson et al., for example, found that about half the 1996 presidential campaign advertisements included at least one misleading statement.[22] Deceitful politicians figure prominently in most explanations of political cynicism and distrust.[23] Pervasive deception certainly discourages respectful attention to politics, and though direct evidence is lacking, probably discourages voting. Finally, public alienation is magnified by media emphasis on conflict.[24] In the end, candidate strategies that irritate or put people off reduce the incidence of participation.

Voters' Reform Priorities   I've noted that campaign finance reform is often seen as an essential, perhaps *the* essential way to restore public confidence in the political process,[25] and polls do often show majority public support for such reforms. A typical poll, conducted by the *New York Times* and CBS News, found that 50 percent believed fundamental changes in the campaign finance system were needed, while 39 percent felt the system needed to be completely rebuilt.[26] But when asked "Whose attempts to buy influence bother you the most?" the largest plurality, 45 percent, identified foreign governments. Only 25 percent identified "American special interest groups" and just 21 percent "wealthy people." Though they support reform, Americans in the aggregate are not quite as bothered, especially by domestic influence-buying, as such 2000 presidential candidates as John McCain, along with many academic, media, and political critics, seem to be.

In fact, campaign finance practices are only one of several features of candidate behavior that trouble citizens, and arguably not the most important. The final 1996 Markle Presidential Election Watch survey, for example, found that campaign finance reform ranked no higher than third in importance to a random national sample on a list of desirable political changes.

Table 7.1 presents the survey question and reports the results. When asked which two of seven options for changing future campaigns would make the biggest positive differences, respondents put two other changes in candidate behaviors: "more honesty and information from the candidates" (57 percent) and "less negative campaigning" (35 percent) in the top two places. Other possible improvements, such as campaign finance reform (25 percent), higher voter turnout (23 percent), a shortened campaign season (19 percent), more informative media coverage (18 percent), and a third party with a real chance to win (20 percent), generated significant but substantially less-popular support, as the percentages indicate.

TABLE 7.1   CITIZEN RANKINGS OF PROSPECTIVE CAMPAIGN CHANGES

As you think about what you like and dislike about this year's campaign, which one of the following changes, if any, do you think would do most to make things better in future elections.

57%—More honesty and information from the candidates
35%—Less negative campaigning
25%—Campaign finance reform
23%—A higher voter turnout
20%—A third party with a real chance to win
19%—A shorter campaign season
18%—More informative news coverage
0%—Other (Specify)
11%—Nothing/Satisfied
2%—Don't know/Refused

Source: Princeton Survey Research Associates, 10/21–11/2/1996, n = 936; Total exceeds 100% due to multiple responses.

The implication for efforts to make campaigns more appealing to prospective voters is obvious: *Change the practices—candidate dissembling and negativity—that citizens identify as most in need of correction.* Such a strategy seems likely to have the greatest *immediate* impact on respect and trust in the political process and perhaps on the willingness to learn and vote.

Remedies   There is a limit to what can be done, short of illegal regulation of free speech or hard-to-muster electoral leverage (discussed later), to force candidates to be as honest, positive, and informative as citizens want them to be. But recent approaches to these ends offer short-term influence potential. One is the "Stand-By-Your-Ad," proposal recently advanced by the Alliance for Better Campaigns.[27] Getting candidates to publicly accept responsibility for their advertising by including their names in the presentation is a way to discourage the worst excesses. A stronger measure is the "Ad Watch" practice, which attaches real and immediate costs to candidate misrepresentation. It involves efforts by TV and print journalists to assess and report on the truthfulness of candidates' advertising. Significantly, ad watches do not require the voluntary cooperation of candidates to be effective. They work instead by publicly stigmatizing the sponsors of misleading ads, which can make the misrepresentation unacceptably costly to candidates. Despite the currently inconclusive state of the scholarly evidence on ad watches, the research-sensitive Pew Task Force on Campaign Reform concluded that they probably do mitigate the impact of misleading campaign discourse, "especially by deterring campaigners from airing misleading or unfair ads."[28]

STEP TWO: STRENGTHEN SITUATIONAL INCENTIVES

The second major reform step is to add to, strengthen, and routinize various situational incentives able to attract attention and increase participation during each election cycle. *Situational incentives are created by things that happen, either by accident or by design, to attract attention, stimulate interest, and potentially to increase learning and voting during particular campaign seasons.* All voter mobilization, intended or not, is situational in this sense. Voters are often mobilized in potentially quite significant, though time-bound ways, for example, by anxiety-provoking circumstances like economic or military crises, and by atypical candidates with appealing styles and/or messages, like John F. Kennedy, Ronald Reagan, Ross Perot, Jesse Ventura, and John McCain.

Interesting Candidates   In 2000, McCain managed to spike primary season turnout. Early primaries like New Hampshire, South Carolina, Michigan, and Arizona, which in some instances doubled their 1996 turnout, were cases in point.[29] Earlier, the iconoclastic former professional wrestler, Jesse "The Body" Ventura had also shown how dramatically novel personalities can attract voters. In a midterm election year that saw the lowest average national midterm turnout since 1942—36.1 percent—the governor's race in the state of Minnesota sparked the highest voter turnout of any state in 1998: 59.5 percent.[30] Minnesota led all states because Ventura's was the first name on the ballot, running on Ross Perot's Reform Party ticket. Exit polls showed that most of Ventura's support came from those under the age of forty. Twelve percent said they would not have voted had there been no alternative to the Republican and Democratic candidates. Most of that vote went to Ventura, who drew equally from women and men to win with 37 percent of the vote in a three-way race.[31]

Debates   More routinizable are events like presidential candidate debates. Their unequaled potential for mobilizing attention and interest in presidential campaigns was noted earlier. They have been regular features of presidential politics since 1976. They have long been known to affect audience attention, interest and learning,[32] and they also influence the magnitude of voting in particular years. These facts make them vital tools for engaging the electorate. But their attention-mobilizing capacity remains situational because it is affected by varying events and participants.

A case in point was the decision of the Commission on Presidential Debates to bar Ross Perot from the 1996 debates. His exclusion reduced interest in the debates and depressed turnout. The 1992 Perot experience shows why. In that year, Perot increased the size of the debate audience. He also "increased turnout by nearly three percentage points. One out of every five Perot supporters would not have voted had Perot not entered the race."[33] He would not have had such an effect on turnout in 1992 had he been denied the exposure provided by the debates.

The debate commission based its 1996 decision to exclude Perot on the conclusion that he lacked a "realistic" chance to win. *This standard is too insensitive to the decisive role debates now play in stimulating mass interest in the campaign.* Given the forty-year decline in participation, attracting public attention is now a greater priority than protecting those that the commission thinks have the best chance to win. This is an especially unfortunate example of the tendency of elite bodies, whether courts, parties, candidate organizations, or blue-ribbon commissions to privilege candidate interests over the interests and wishes of the mass public.

One way to ensure that debates attract the largest possible audience would be to include any candidate, major party nominee or not, whom 51 percent or more of a national sample says *should* participate. This standard would be unlikely to include more than three participants in any given year. Under this rule, Perot would have qualified in 1996.

Partisan Mobilization   Other potentially routinizable events, which are closer than the above to the traditional understanding of mobilization, include the efforts of political parties, particular candidate campaigns, social movements and interest groups to mobilize citizens via get-out-the vote and voter education efforts in particular years. The fairly standard techniques, as well as the enduring value of such mobilization strategies, were both especially well-illustrated by the "unprecedented" and unexpectedly successful labor mobilization of "tens of thousands of union households" that defeated Proposition 226 in the June 2, 1998, California primary. If successful, the proposition would have forced unions to get written permission from their members before spending dues money on political advocacy. Even some of labor's conservative Republican critics, able practitioners of the same techniques, were said to have been impressed by the effectiveness of a union campaign that featured a massive grass-roots mobilization of 659,000 phone calls, contacts by precinct walkers of more than 600,000 union members and their families, visits to 18,000 work sites, more than 500,000 pieces of mail sent to union households, the use of television ads linking the proposition to conservative, antiunion outsiders, and the identification of some 24,000 new activists who will be used in a campaign to register new voters in union households in the fall campaign.[34]

Traditional mobilization by political parties has been in decline.[35] Political parties have grown comfortable with the low-turnout environment.[36] But there are signs that mobilization is coming back into favor. Inspired by the California labor example, both major parties in the days before the 1998 midterm elections mounted "vast telephone, mailing and advertising drives to prod millions of loyalists to the polls." In California alone, Republicans made three and a half million phone calls to their partisans, while Democrats mailed slate cards to three million of their voters.[37] The emphasis on partisan mobilization continued in 2000 and 2002.

Nonpartisan Mobilization   By broadening turnout beyond the intense partisans within each political party, mass partisan mobilizations not only increase participation, but also help to mitigate the ideological polarization that now characterizes American politics.[38] But party-based mobilization is not enough.

Missing and sorely needed is an established, nonpartisan mobilizing voice that speaks to the people on behalf of the electoral process in an appeal to the civic duty sentiment. The only voices now broadcast widely enough during campaigns to have a chance to "move the masses" are those of candidates, moneyed interests, and television journalists. Establishing a credible, nonpartisan voice that issues a strong plea to the 70 percent that identifies voting as the primary citizen duty would do more than merely reinforce the roughly 50 percent of eligibles who already vote (see Table 4.1 on page 71). *Most importantly, it would prick the consciences of those within the additional 20 percent who pay lip service to voting in response to pollsters' questions, but who do not regularly show up at the polls.* Their avowal of the importance of voting implies an important measure of guilty receptivity to mobilizing appeals. That makes them the most promising target for efforts to increase turnout. It is realistic to expect that a goodly number of current no-shows would heed a nonpartisan call that was as frequently repeated as the advertising for any candidate or brand name product.

The value of nonpartisan mobilization was convincingly demonstrated in a recent series of field experiments involving some 30,000 eligible voters and conducted in New Haven, Connecticut. Using "mild" nonpartisan exhortations to vote, Gerber and Green[39] found that face-to-face contacts increased turnout by about 7 percentage points, leaflet distributions generated 5 percent increases, and a series of mailings yielded a 1.5 percent increase. Gerber and Green speculate that nonpartisan appeals like those used in New Haven are effective because they have the credibility of public service messages: "People who believe in the importance of electoral participation are inspired by messages that encourage them to go to the polls, much in the same way that periodic blood donors are inspired by Red Cross appeals."[40] Extrapolating from their own mobilization research expenses and their experimental findings, these authors estimate that using the most cost-effective technology to reach all 150 million registered voters would cost about $75 million (a tiny fraction of total campaign spending in 2000) and generate a 4 percent voting age population turnout increase.

A novel nonpartisan, not-for-profit effort to address low turnout in general and in particular among the lowest-voting eighteen- to twenty-four-year-old group was mounted by former Clinton Press Secretary Michael D. McCurry and former Republican consultant Doug Bailey in advance of the 2002 midterm elections. Called "Freedom's Answer," the initiative mobilized thousands of high school students in a nationwide voter drive that included their teachers and others to produce what they hoped would be the largest midterm election turnout in the nation's history. The engagement of high school students was intended to lay the foundation for a new civics curriculum that McCurry and Bailey described as absent from the nation's schools. By engaging students in school, where systematic organization and instruction could augment the initiative, and by enlisting people who were not yet of voting age, the founders hoped to provide an experience that would prove to the participants and to successive generations of future voters that young people can make a difference. The experiment tested the proposition that the taste of power an impact on the vote would provide could be an enduring incentive for future political engagement.[41]

STEP THREE: REINVENTING CITIZENSHIP

Citizens, it is fair to say, are now largely passive participants in a process that, while nominally intended to privilege their interests, instead better serves the interests of candidates and journalists. Removing barriers to participation and strengthening situational incentives are necessary, but ultimately insufficient steps to rectifying the interest imbalance. If citizens are ever to get more consistent control over the content and tone of campaigns a great many of them must also be better *equipped* and more *willing* to use the leverage they have. That requires more ambitious changes than anything we have considered to this point; changes that, as warned, are not quickly or easily obtained. Three in particular require attention.

A New Template   Needed first is a campaign template that specifies, along lines set out in Chapter 1, how a satisfactory presidential campaign should work and how candidates, media, and voters must perform to achieve the vision. Further, the template must be widely publicized, well understood, and accepted. A recent family of political experiments represents worthy efforts to supply such a template.

The most comprehensive experiment to date, the Minnesota Compact Model was an agreement among the major campaign players in that state to observe certain standards of behavior during the 1996 fight for election to the U.S. Senate. Sponsored and widely publicized by a coalition of academic, civic, business, and media groups, the Minnesota Compact was endorsed by 283 candidates for state and local offices in the 1996 election. It clearly described the responsibilities of candidates (e.g., avoid false and misleading attacks), the news media (e.g., identify voter concerns and candidate responses; avoid "horse race" focus), and citizens (e.g., accept responsibility to participate in informal discussion and to watch debates) in the electoral process, and invited clear commitments to such norms from the major campaign actors in advance of the campaign. Tested was the proposition that prior clarity and agreement on responsibilities by the key actors would lead to cooperation on all sides, and make public expectations a more powerful corrective force.

Newspaper coverage of the Senate race between Paul Wellstone and Rudy Boschwitz did avoid an excessive focus on strategy and tactics and offered sustained coverage of issues. But Boschwitz, behind in the polls, eventually abandoned the compact, putting up attack ads against Wellstone. Surveys suggest that these ads may have backfired, with voters rejecting the Boschwitz campaign as too negative and unfair. "It is possible," wrote Paul Taylor, "that the compact contributed to an atmosphere where voters could deliver such a judgment."[42] To the extent that Boschwitz's defeat could be construed as punishment for his attacks, Minnesota voters had taken a significant step toward attaching costs to attack strategies.

By positioning voters as enforcers of clearly defined rules, compacts show how campaigns can be structured to create citizen leverage. They are also likely to heighten citizens' feelings of efficacy and of responsibility for the process, which can reinforce the desire to participate. These are the core elements of an effective citizen portfolio. And that is what makes the compact model an especially promising resource for the "reprogramming" of adults and the political initiation of the young, whether in actual campaigns, traditional school civics courses, or in election-centered outreach programs such as Kids Voting USA.[43]

Since the Minnesota Compact, the "codes of conduct" idea has been deployed in several state political races by the Institute for Global Ethics' Project on Campaign Conduct. Their 1998 and 2000 efforts focused on Washington and Ohio, and in 2002 the project expanded to forty congressional districts in nineteen states (www.campaignconduct.org). It remains to be seen if such efforts will continue to progress, state-by-state, from the status of occasional "demonstration projects" to that of "established national practice," as is needed to make possible a shift of power toward citizens.

A New Mandate for Voters   The second prerequisite to greater popular control of campaigns is that the citizen-voter job description be expanded; along lines suggested but not sufficiently elaborated by the Minnesota Compact. In the compact, as in regular civic life, the citizen portfolio is incomplete. It does not reliably motivate the kind of action needed to bring regular "pro-quality" pressure to bear on candidates and media. Before citizens can be credibly threatening enough to evoke both substance and civility they must not only become more dependable learners and voters; *they must also agree to police the process.* This is the missing link. It is the most important corrective proposed in this book. It also entails a far different civic self-concept than most Americans now embrace.

Current Expectations   Table 7.2 (on page 122), which reports the campaign season expectations citizens have of candidates and media, identify performance standards that, if met, would improve campaigns. The expectations amount to nascent codes of conduct, though adjustments are needed. One omission is a lack of any expectations for media truth-testing of candidates and avoidance of overly critical reporting. The most important shortcoming, however, is that the expectations that do appear are not widely enough shared. None is endorsed by more than 30 percent of poll respondents.

The Expanded Citizen Portfolio   The election-season expectations that citizens have for themselves, however, are the most problematic. As reported in Table 4.1 on page 71, they are to register and vote (70 percent) and to stay informed (25 percent). These expectations evince one clear shortcoming

TABLE 7.2   CITIZENS' EXPECTATIONS OF CANDIDATES AND MEDIA
(1996 PRESIDENTIAL ELECTION CAMPAIGN)

What would you say presidential candidates should do in a campaign in order to help voters make a good voting choice?

Character/Honesty	
Be truthful	30%
Be consistent	8
Information	
Explain/clarify issue stands	13
Publish plans/set timetable	11
Stick to issues	10
Conduct	
Avoid mudslinging/negative campaigning	14

In a presidential election, TV news shows and newspapers have an important role to play in providing information and other services to voters. What would you say is the most important kind of information they should provide to voters?

Explanation	
Interpretation/analysis of facts	25%
Information	
Issues/platform in general	21
Issues specifics	14
Candidates' background	9
General information	7
Conduct	
Avoid biased reporting	8

Source: Princeton Survey Research Associates, 10/21–11/02/1996; n = 1,881.

and one glaring omission. The shortcoming is that too few identify learning, or following the campaign, as responsibilities. The omission is that none identify enforcement as a component of the citizen portfolio. These are precisely the blanks to be filled and the gaps to be closed if citizen leverage on campaigns is to increase. To hold candidates and media accountable for their campaign conduct, citizens must continuously monitor candidate and media behavior for compliance with expectations (surveillance). Further, votes must be cast, and media consumption decisions made, in part with the intent to punish noncompliance in mind (enforcement).

Surveillance in this context means watching to ensure that the codes are observed. What must voters know in order to enforce the codes? There are various kinds of political learning and many convincing arguments in support of the necessity and desirability of each.[44] But for the purposes at hand, *three campaign-specific bodies of information are most relevant: the consensual policy priorities of the nation at the time, the policy proposals of specific candidates, and the ongoing campaign performances of those candidates and the news organizations that cover them.*

The reasons are obvious. Citizens who are unaware of the bipartisan consensus as to what the national policy priorities are cannot be competent appraisers of the plausibility and relevance to national priorities of specific candidates' platforms, nor are they equipped to signal authoritative demands that candidates address national rather than self-interested priorities. Similarly, ignorance of the evolving candidate issue discussion and debate makes it impossible to notice shifts in candidate compliance with the policy expectations of voters. And ignorance of news accounts of the tenor of the candidates' campaign styles and strategies, the content and tone of candidate advertising, and the overall nature and content of media campaign coverage, obviously neutralizes voters as effective constraints against repellent tactics or less-than-useful coverage patterns.

To press for a selective program of campaign-season learning is not to ask for more than ordinary people can deliver. It is to ask for reasonable, relatively low-cost investments already exceeded by many members of a civic culture known in the aggregate as more politically involved outside the electoral sphere than other Western democracies.[45] The irony, and the challenge to architects of a new citizen portfolio, is that a population that is increasingly well educated in general terms[46] *avoids* learning when it comes to politics.[47]

The biggest challenge, however, is to inculcate a sense of responsibility for punishing political misbehavior. This involves a quantum expansion of civic self-definition beyond mere "voter" to the more formidable role of "enforcer." Still, *the idea that citizens should assume such a role in their own interest is far from novel. It is implicit in various strands of democratic theory, especially "protective" democratic theory, discussed in Chapter 4, which is focused on mechanisms for ensuring the accountability of governors to the governed.*[48]

The problem is that the passive habits of American voters do not square with the assertive mindset needed for enforcement. Few citizens now think of their expectations as authoritative demands or potential threats. Nor do they think of themselves as enforcers. For most, politics is something practiced by other people, for the benefit of other people, with little relevance to their lives. Elsewhere I have argued that this widespread *psychological distance* from political affairs and the associated lack of any sense of ownership or stake in the process underlies the tendency to respond to political discontent with "exit" rather than "voice." Nothing, it seems, is more deeply rooted in the contemporary American political culture.[49]

Civic Duty Revisited   The hardest part of the effort to improve the average quality of presidential campaigns is getting citizens to care enough to assert themselves in quiet as well as troubled times. I suggested in the Preface that the only conceivable way to make this happen is to revive the now-defunct practice of explicitly cultivating the *civic duty* sentiment in each new generation of Americans. The psychologically distant must be brought close; the new citizen portfolio taken to heart. That is the third essential change.

By civic duty, I mean a learned disposition to view such activities as voting and norm enforcement as *responsibilities*, fulfillment of which yields intrinsic satisfaction, or "psychic reward."[50] "Duty exists to the extent that people are willing to honor obligations in the absence of [external] social rewards for doing so. . . . Duty is the way by which people cope with the free rider problem in the absence of coercion."[51]

As long noted by public choice theorists,[52] citizens who measure the value of voting by whether it can affect the outcome will rarely have reason to bother. Duty is the one disposition consistently able to override the lure of nonparticipation. Instilled by families and schools, civic duty becomes, for many, an internal commitment that is *strong enough to impel action independently of external, situational incentives*. The stronger the sense of duty, the greater the likelihood of voting.[53] For those who feel responsible, inaction is a source of guilt, while action is satisfying. Without such psychic pressure, the benefits of dutiful action can never exceed the costs.

The Fraying of Civic Duty   But while lip service to voting endures, we have seen that turnout continues to decline, especially among the young. There has been a sharp drop in civic engagement among those in what Miller and Shanks[54] call the "Post–New Deal" generation that entered the voting age population between 1968 and 1992. The lower turnout and the markedly less-positive feelings toward the value of citizenship that characterize the younger in comparison with older generations of eligible voters[55] demonstrates the failure of basic civic training. Data from the 1996 Markle survey (not reported in tables) show that "personal importance of voting" and "interest in presidential politics" scores are significantly lower for younger compared to older voters. For example, *while 83 percent of those between the ages of 55 and 64 described voting in the 1996 election as "very important" to them, only 54 percent of those between the ages of 18 and 24 did the same.* And only 13 percent of the younger group described themselves as "very interested" in presidential politics, compared to 50 percent of the older group.

Reviving Regime Support   The urgent need to connect politically with the young is reason enough to rethink the goals and upgrade the methods of civic education. It is worth noting that the move after World War II away from "nation building" (which stressed loyalty and duty) to "critical thinking" (which features independence and skepticism) content for civic education[56] fits the generational drop in turnout identified by such scholars as Miller and Shanks. This strongly suggests that the turn away from normative instruction in loyalty and duty was a fundamental mistake. Needed is a systematic renewal of efforts to instill regime support, accompanied by participatory activities designed to reinforce it.

How can this be made to happen? This is not the place for a detailed blueprint, but the basics have already been introduced and discussed throughout this book. They include a substantive core of instruction in democratic theory—particularly the teaching that the American electoral process represents history's best effort to equip ordinary people with the means to protect their interests. Protective democracy is the ideal that justifies a call for individuals to accept responsibility for doing what is necessary to make the system work.

Apropos of the argument in Chapter 4, allegiance to the American electoral process must be built by cultivating identification with the normative ideal, and then by reinforcing that identification through participation in electoral activities. Required is exposure to both the ideal and its reinforcement through the life cycle. In families, the message is communicated through discussion and parental modeling and reinforced through family volunteer activities. In schools, the ideal is taught, and then reinforced by political activities organized around ongoing campaigns, as is now done by the Kids Voting USA program (see Endnote 43) or the Freedom's Answer get-out-the-vote effort mentioned earlier. Schools should also feature case studies of the successful applications of the compact model and codes of conduct experiments, along with illustrations like those in Chapter 6 of citizens demanding results and either getting them or inflicting consequences. Examples like Minnesota actually negotiating codes of conduct and then voters holding candidates like Rudy Boschwitz accountable are particularly valuable. It is advisable that all such activities be kept separate from partisanship or any identification with political parties. This fits the characteristics of the young, who tend to be independent, less committed than their elders to political parties or doctrines, and more eager to see new approaches to politics.[57]

How is the sense of political responsibility to be nurtured? Just as other life duties are taught. Role models and teachers, by their words and deeds, point the way. In this case, they must exhort their charges to accept the challenge of protecting the quality of elections. Voting alone is no longer enough. Vigilance and enforcement are equally important. Like voting, they must be portrayed as matters of high personal obligation.

Conclusion

The grand purpose of all democratic reform was expressed by Alexis de Tocqueville in a June 13, 1835, letter to a friend: ". . . the true goal that friends of democracy must aim for . . . [is] to place the majority of citizens in a position to govern and make them capable of governing . . . to bring modern societies to this point by degree seems to me the only way to save them from barbarism and slavery.[58]

In modern mass democracies, citizens govern not directly, but by getting meaningful control of elected representatives during the seasons of maximum citizen influence: elections. That, I have argued, requires updating the capacity of citizens to command the respect of those who seek their votes.

The point of democratic forms like secret ballots, regular voting, and competition for election is precisely to ensure respect for the will of the people. But these venerable instruments of accountability, while necessary, have not been sufficient. In the absence of vigilant, knowledgeable, and purposive voters, sophisticated manipulation has enabled candidates to obtain by guile, under the protective cover of these ancient democratic forms, the very thing the forms were created to prevent: preferential treatment for the interests of elites.

I have tried to show that the antidote—a long-term program that integrates selective campaign reform with targeted citizen development to bring forth a more proactive kind of voter—is operationally feasible. But as Tocqueville observed, we cannot expect to bring citizens to this point quickly and easily. It can happen only in time and by degree.

Notes

1. Morris P. Fiorina and Paul E. Peterson, *The New American Democracy* (Boston: Allyn and Bacon, 1998), p. 177.
2. Geneva Overholser, "America Needs a Popular Revolt," *Austin American-Statesman*, 16 December 1998, p. A-19.
3. Francis X. Clines, "Most Doubt a Resolve to Change Campaign Financing, Poll Finds," *New York Times*, 8 April 1997, p. A-1.
4. Alison Mitchell, "Campaign Finance Bill Wins Final Approval in Congress and Bush Says He'll Sign It," *New York Times*, 21 March 2002, p. A-1.
5. Don Van Natta, Jr., and Richard A. Oppel, Jr., "Parties Create Ways to Avoid Soft Money Ban," *New York Times*, 2 November 2002, p. A-1.
6. Center for Media and Public Affairs, press release, Washington, D.C., spring 1997.
7. Larry M. Bartels et al., "Campaign Reform: Insights and Evidence," Report of the Task Force on Campaign Reform (Princeton, NJ: Princeton University, 1998), p. 30.
8. See, for example, Larry M. Bartels et al., "Campaign Reform: Insights and Evidence," Report of the Task Force on Campaign Reform (Princeton, NJ: Princeton University, 1998), p. 31; Charles M. Firestone and Amy Korzick Garmer, eds., *Digital Broadcasting and the Public Interest* (Washington, D.C.: The Aspen Institute, 1998).
9. Jill Abramson. "Election Panel Refuses to Order Repayments by Clinton and Dole," *New York Times*, 11 December 1998, p. A-1.
10. Charles M. Firestone and Amy Korzick Garmer, eds., *Digital Broadcasting and the Public Interest* (Washington, D.C.: The Aspen Institute, 1998), p. ix.

11. Geneva Overholser, "What Readers Want, What Readers Get," *Austin American-Statesman*, 13 February 2000, p. H-3.
12. "Motor Voters Register but Lack Drive at the Polls," *Dallas Morning News*, 21 June 1997, p. A-8.
13. "Why Citizens Shun the Polling Booth: An Interview with Curtis B. Gans," *The Public Perspective*, February/March 1997, p. 43.
14. Larry M. Bartels et al., "Campaign Reform: Insights and Evidence," Report of the Task Force on Campaign Reform (Princeton, NJ: Princeton University, 1998), p. 30.
15. Ibid., p. 43.
16. Richard A. Lau and Lee Sigelman, "The Effectiveness of Negative Political Advertising: A Literature Review" (paper presented at the American University Conference on Improving Campaign Conduct, Washington, D.C., April 1998).
17. John Harwood and Jeanne Cummings, "Tactical Retreat One Likely Casualty of the Clinton Years: The Scandal Gambit," *Wall Street Journal*, 11 December 1998, p. A-1.
18. Greg Hitt, "Specific-Issue Ads in Presidential Battle Are Running at a Record-Setting Pace," *Wall Street Journal*, 17 March 2000, p. A-20.
19. Robert C. Luskin and Christopher N. Bratcher, "Negative Campaigning, Partisanship, and Turnout" (paper presented at the annual meeting of the American Political Science Association, Chicago, 1995); Stephen Ansolabehere and Shanto Iyengar, *Going Negative: How Political Advertisements Shrink and Polarize the Electorate* (New York: Free Press, 1995).
20. James Dao, "Seeking Upset, Bradley Enlists Unlikely Model," *New York Times*, 27 December 1999, p. A-1.
21. Bruce Buchanan, *Renewing Presidential Politics: Campaigns, Media, and the Public Interest* (Lanham, MD: Rowman and Littlefield, 1996), pp. 101–103.
22. Kathleen Hall Jamieson et al., *1996: Better or Worse?* (Annenberg Public Policy Center, University of Pennsylvania, November 1996), p. 6.
23. Sissela Bok, *Lying: Moral Choice in Public and Private Life* (New York: Vintage, 1979), p. 184.
24. See Joseph N. Cappella and Kathleen Hall Jamieson, *Spiral of Cynicism: The Press and the Public Good* (New York: Oxford, 1997); S. Robert Lichter and Richard E. Noyes, *Good Intentions Make Bad News: Why Americans Hate Campaign Journalism* (Lanham, MD: Rowman and Littlefield, 1995).
25. Citizen's Research Foundation, *New Realities, New Thinking*, Report of the Task Force on Campaign Finance Reform (Los Angeles, CA: University of Southern California, March 1997).
26. Francis X. Clines, "Most Doubt a Resolve to Change Campaign Financing, Poll Finds," *New York Times*, 8 April 1997, p. A-1.
27. The Alliance is a public interest group, directed by Paul Taylor, that seeks to "improve elections by promoting voluntary, realistic standards of campaign conduct, discourse and coverage." See their Issue Briefs #2 and #3 in their Information Kit, available at 529 14th Street NW, suite 320, Washington, D.C. 20045.
28. Larry M. Bartels et al., "Campaign Reform: Insights and Evidence," Report of the Task Force on Campaign Reform (Princeton, NJ: Princeton University, 1998), pp. 18–19.
29. Adam Clymer, "McCain Factor Quiets Talk of Dwindling Turnout," *New York Times*, 26 February 2000, p. A-11.
30. Richard L. Berke, "Democrats' Gains Dispel Notion That the G.O.P. Benefits from Low Turnout," *New York Times*, 6 November 1998, p. A-22.
31. Clarence Page, "An Independent Streak: Generation X Does Vote, but Not Like Mom or Dad," *Austin American-Statesman*, 12 November 1998, p. A-15.
32. Kathleen Hall Jamieson and David S. Birdsell, *Presidential Debates* (New York: Oxford, 1988).
33. Dean Lacy and Barry C. Burden, "The Vote-Stealing and Turnout Effects of Ross Perot in the 1992 Presidential Election," *American Journal of Political Science* 43 (1999), pp. 233–255.
34. Glenn Burkins, "Union Win on California Dues Notification Issue May Offer Successful Strategy for Fall Elections," *Wall Street Journal*, 4 June 1998, p. A-20.
35. Steven J. Rosenstone and John Mark Hansen, *Mobilization, Participation, and Democracy in America* (New York: Macmillan, 1993), p. 213.
36. Lowi and Ginsberg argue that "even with America's personal registration rules, higher levels of political participation could be achieved if competing political forces made a serious effort to mobilize voters. Unfortunately, however, contending political forces in the United States have found ways of attacking their opponents that do not require them to

engage in voter mobilization, and many prefer to use these methods than to endeavor to bring more voters to the polls. The low levels of popular mobilization that are typical of contemporary American politics are very much a function of the way politics is conducted in the United States today." Theodore J. Lowi and Benjamin Ginsberg, *American Government: Freedom and Power*, brief 5th ed. (New York: W. W. Norton, 1998), p. 264. Certain low turnout groups suffer as a result. Because "poor Americans are voting less and less," for example, the Democrats are able to ignore their interests and better compete with Republicans for centrist positions on such issues as the budget surplus. See Christopher Georges, "Democrats' Plans to Sit on the Projected Surplus Deeply Divides Liberals Outside, Inside Congress," *Wall Street Journal*, 10 June 1998, p. A-20.

37. Richard L. Berke, "Parties Beginning Enormous Efforts to Prompt Voters," *New York Times*, 25 October 1998, p. A-1.

38. Jackie Calmes, "House Divided: Why Congress Hews to the Party Lines on Impeachment," *Wall Street Journal*, 16 December 1998, p. A-1.

39. Alan Gerber and Donald Green, "The Effects of Canvassing, Leafleting, and Direct Mail on Voter Turnout: A Field Experiment" (paper presented at the annual meeting of the Midwest Political Science Association, Chicago, IL, 1999).

40. Ibid., p. 21.

41. "Civics Lesson for Students in Vote Drive," *New York Times*, 2 November 2002, p. A-12.

42. Paul Taylor, "Case Study: The Minnesota Compact" (Washington, D.C.: Alliance for Better Campaigns, June 15, 1998).

43. Kids Voting USA is a nonprofit, nonpartisan organization with branch offices in forty states and activities in 6,000 schools across the United States. It reaches some 5 million students in grades K–12 with programs organized around election campaigns in progress. The curriculum includes use of newspapers, family and in-class discussions, and community events. The Kids Voting USA slogan is "Voters Rule!" Research on the program shows that it stimulates interest, discussion, learning, and newspaper reading. It is also said to increase parental voting rates by 5 to 10 percent. Larry M. Bartels et al., "Campaign Reform: Insights and Evidence," Report of the Task Force on Campaign Reform (Princeton, NJ: Princeton University, 1998), p. 39.

44. Cf., Norman H. Nie, Jane Junn, and Kenneth Stehlik-Barry, *Education and Democratic Citizenship in America* (Chicago, IL: University of Chicago Press, 1996); Michael X. Delli Carpini and Scott Keeter, *What Americans Know about Politics and Why It Matters* (New Haven, CT: Yale University Press, 1996).

45. Sidney Verba, Kay Lehman Schlozman, and Henry E. Brady, *Voice and Equality: Civic Voluntarism in American Politics* (Cambridge, MA: Harvard University Press, 1995).

46. Cf., Steven J. Rosenstone and John Mark Hansen, *Mobilization, Participation, and Democracy in America* (New York: Macmillan, 1993), p. 214; Steven A. Holmes, "A Generally Healthy Nation Emerges in a New Census Report about Life in America," *New York Times*, 13 October 1994, p. A-13.

47. Paul M. Sniderman, "The New Look in Public Opinion Research," in *Political Science: The State of the Discipline II*, ed. Ada W. Finifer (Washington, D.C.: American Political Science Association, 1993).

48. David Held, *Models of Democracy*, 2nd ed. (Stanford, CA: Stanford University Press, 1996), pp. 88–89.

49. Bruce Buchanan, *Renewing Presidential Politics: Campaigns, Media, and the Public Interest* (Lanham, MD: Rowman and Littlefield, 1996), pp. 21–37.

50. Morris P. Fiorina and Paul E. Peterson, *The New American Democracy* (Boston: Allyn and Bacon, 1998), p. 175.

51. James Q. Wilson, *The Moral Sense* (New York: Free Press, 1993).

52. Cf., Anthony Downs, *An Economic Theory of Democracy* (New York: Harper & Row, 1957); William H. Riker and Peter C. Ordeshook, "A Theory of the Calculus of Voting," *American Political Science Review* 62 (1968), pp. 25–42.

53. Angus Campbell, Philip E. Converse, Warren E. Miller, and Donald E. Stokes, *The American Voter: An Abridgement* (New York: Wiley, 1964).

54. Warren E. Miller and J. Merrill Shanks, *The New American Voter* (Cambridge, MA: Harvard University Press, 1996).

55. Wendy M. Rahn, "Generations and American National Identity: A Data Essay" (paper presented at the Communication in the Future of Democracy Workshop, Annenberg Center, Washington D.C., May 8–9, 1998).
56. Morris Janowitz, *Reconstructing Patriotism* (Chicago: University of Chicago Press, 1983).
57. Michele Mitchell, *A New Kind of Party Animal: How the Young Are Tearing up the American Political Landscape* (New York: Simon & Schuster, 1998).
58. Andre Jardin, *Tocqueville: A Biography* (New York: Farrar, Straus, Giroux, 1988), p. 235.

INDEX